The

ANNUAL REVIEW

Number 18—2019

Editor's Note

Longtime readers of the *Tennessee Williams Annual Review* will notice that the cover of the 2019 issue deviates from the journal's standard design. Instead of occupying the center of the cover, this year's image, a portrait of Edwina Dakin Williams flanked by her young children Rose and Tom—but without their father (and without son Dakin, who was not yet born)—wraps around the spine, moving Rose to the back and inviting readers to imagine the design as a graphic representation of the complex Williams family dynamics.

Edwina's version of some of those dynamics composes the compelling first act of this issue: the only known entries from her diary, written between 1931 and 1934, are collected and published here in their entirety for the first time. In them readers will find her lived account of the marital conflict that will appear, aesthetically transformed, in some of Williams's best-known works, including *The Glass Menagerie* and *Suddenly Last Summer*. As the biographer and critic John Bak makes clear in his introduction, the diary entries provide a wealth of material for the life-and-works approaches that have illuminated the Williams oeuvre. Of interest here as well is the complex portrait that emerges of this strong-willed and long-suffering mother—substantially different from the somewhat saccharine and unconvincingly obtuse version of herself that Edwina offered the public in her memoir, *Remember Me to Tom*. This newly revealed Edwina is a much more plausible model for *Menagerie*'s Amanda Wingfield, one of the playwright's most intricately conceived and intriguing characters, a deeply disappointed and fiercely loving matriarch, the bright if destructive sun around whom her children endlessly orbit.

The idea of new angles shaking up existing views provides a through line for this issue. Julie Vatain-Corfdir breaks new ground with her reassessment of Jean Cocteau and Raymond Rouleau's quickly panned 1949 Paris production of *A Streetcar Named Desire* (*Un tramway nommé Désir*), whose playtext was adapted by Cocteau, one of France's most celebrated literary and theatrical figures. Idiosyncratic and rife with mistranslations (intentional and otherwise), the adaptation was mocked, but Vatain-Corfdir's impressive archival study shows it to be "a revelatory case study for the reception of American drama in France"—a production whose perceived oddities in fact identified not only the elements of *Streetcar* that would eventually succeed with French audiences but also where the difficulties lay.

Also offering a revisionary angle is Michael Hooper's study of homoeroticism in Williams's painting. Hooper understands visual art to have been much more than a hobby for the playwright: the product of many years of not unfruitful devotion, Williams's oeuvre of paintings provides crucial insight into the creative process of an artist famous for incorporating the visual into the literary and vice versa. The essay examines three late-era canvases in depth, demonstrating the ways that Williams's representations of the homoerotic go beyond simple voyeurism and grapple with many of the themes and tensions that surface more obliquely in the dramas that made him one of the best-known and most popular writers in the United States during the 1950s and '60s. Hooper shines a bright light on an aspect of the playwright's life previously known for the most part only to his friends and family, adding another chapter to the collective biography that is key to Williams studies.

On his death, in 1983, Williams left behind not only a wealth of published writing but a huge number of unpublished literary texts—some constituting finished works, some in various unfinished stages or fragments. This legacy poses challenges for Williams scholars and calls for complex judgments of artistic value and relevance. Which plays deserve editing, publication, and performance? Which stories, poems, and essays, if published, revise his reputation in useful ways or throw new, important light on themes already explored in his better-known works? Do any of these writings offer insight not only into the author and his oeuvre but also into his broader historical context, especially into literary traditions in the southern United States and the nation as a whole? Tom Mitchell's study of three early, unpublished Williams texts foregrounds their direct engagement with racial issues not often broached openly in Williams's published work. Mitchell's study introduces Williams scholars to texts they otherwise would likely not know, pointing out ways in which the playwright's early approach to race fleshes out our understanding of his evolving artistic sensibility and cultural politics, which his published canon leaves tantalizingly incomplete.

The issue concludes with a review of two recently published books that investigate the influence of Williams's professional and personal life on the publisher James Laughlin and on two generations of a family tangentially connected with the playwright's youth. The *Review* is dedicated, along with the larger community of Williams scholars, to furthering these intriguingly connected projects.

R. Barton Palmer

2019

Edwina Dakin Williams's Diary Entries, 1931 to 1934: An Introduction

== *John S. Bak*

S cholars and devotees of Tennessee Williams are well aware that the playwright's homelife as a child was anything but harmonious, especially after the family moved to St. Louis and Williams's father, Cornelius (or C.C.), traded his drummer's life for a desk job. Williams repeatedly drew from his storehouse of toxic family memories to populate and dramatize his many plays, short stories, and nonfiction pieces, and the texts' dramatis personae feature recurring types: the abusive father (C.C.); the smothering mother (Edwina); the fragile sister (Rose); the slighted brother (Dakin); and the trapped son (Tom). Five characters in search of a playwright, again and again and again.

This same dramatis personae appears in Edwina Williams's diary, reproduced here for the first time in its fragmented entirety. The playwright materializes as Tom, the Jekyll to Tennessee's soon-to-be-released Hyde, the shy, absent-minded college boy who breaks his glasses (yet again), who prefers life on the other side of the tracks, and who would like finally to stand up to his father but never does.

The limekiln that was the Williams's Enright Avenue apartment during the early 1930s, when Edwina wrote this diary, altered several lives and contributed to the destruction of the family, but it also generated the angst and longing in Williams that would infuse his signature work. There were, of course, the occasional respites for Williams from this tension at home, like summers at Lake Taneycomo in the Ozarks, visits to his grandparents in Clarksdale or Memphis, and a nearly two-month-long tour of Europe with his grandfather's parishioners. But until he found financial independence with the success of *The Glass Menagerie* in 1945, Williams was always forced to move back home to St. Louis.

Williams's first real escape came in September 1929, a week before departing for Columbia, Missouri, to start his first year of college. As Williams wrote in a letter to his grandfather:

> I am leaving for school exactly one week from today and I am awfully busy making the final preparations; going to the dentist, getting clothes and all other necessary equipment. Mother is going up with me to spend one day to see that I am properly settled. She acts as though I were leaving for war instead of for college. (*Selected Letters* 1: 28)

About this departure, Lyle Leverich, the author of Williams's authoritative biography, quipped, "In truth, Tom was moving out of the war zone, and for him at least the next three years would be a blessed truce" (101).

The thirty-six handwritten pages of Edwina's diary collected here together for the first time in print fragmentarily document these warring years from 1931, when Williams was preparing to return to Columbia for his third year, to 1934, when he was living back home permanently after his father denied him his final year in the journalism program at the University of Missouri. The collection is less a diary, in fact, and more a list of charges, for Edwina was not keeping an emotional record of her or her children's struggle in the early years of the Depression as much as she was setting down on paper her husband's selfish and violent mistreatment of the family that she felt he had grown to despise. While her son did occasionally escape, Edwina could not, and her diary is to a certain extent her version of *The Glass Menagerie*, written nearly a decade before her son began tapping into his own lived experiences at home for literary material to exorcise the family's demons and assuage his own mounting guilt for having abandoned Rose to battle her parents alone: *Summer at the Lake* (1939); *At Liberty* (1939); *The Dark Room* (1939); "Blue Roses and the Polar Star" (1941); "Portrait of a Girl in Glass" (1941); *The Front Porch Girl* or *If You Breathe, It Breaks* (1941); and, of course, *The Gentleman Caller* (1943).

Perhaps in keeping this diary Edwina was prescient of her son's future greatness and wanted to tell her side of the family story before Tom did.

Perhaps she needed the emotional release of articulating her grievances, as southern propriety forbade her from taking a confidant for such a purpose (though it seems she did tell C.C.'s boss, Paul Jamison, quite a bit about her troubled marriage).[1] Or, perhaps, she was documenting events to use later as evidence in a divorce proceeding, with which her husband had repeatedly threatened her. In one divorce case from 1929, for example, "repeating notes from a diary or journal" that "described abusive incident after abusive incident, both physical and otherwise" was not only admissible in court but even swayed the judge's final decision (albeit hesitantly) in the wife's favor (Snell 20).[2] Edwina and C.C. never officially divorced, but they did agree to a legal separation in 1946.

It is impossible to be sure of Edwina's motivation, but it is irrefutable that she was following a trend since the Victorian age to keep a diary not just to record intimate secrets[3] or promote "self-examination" but also "to foster, materialise and reflect an authorial persona" (Millim 2). That persona eventually comes through loud and clear in her published memoir, *Remember Me to Tom*, in which some of the details of this diary make a brief, albeit expurgated, appearance. Edwina notes in the memoir, "I kept a diary which I later destroyed when I read it and realized the horror of the things happening in my daily life. But at the time, I had to write of my husband's brutality or I could not have endured it" (59). Some of the events recorded in these entries are corroborated by her two sons in their separate memoirs,[4] but such cross-examination of her version of the facts is distracting at best, dangerous at worst. At the very least, it risks obscuring much of what is interesting about the text—starting with Edwina's own particular brand of forlorn southern belle sensationalism,[5] which finds its way into Amanda Wingfield and Blanche DuBois and other quintessentially Williams characters.

Details of the fragments published here suggest that Edwina's claim in her memoir to have destroyed the diary was not a fib, at least not entirely. She may well have thought that she destroyed the entire diary, and she may indeed have burned or torn up much of it—a metaphorical self-lobotomy, as if she were both Catharine and Violet Venable in *Suddenly Last Summer*, the trauma victim and the controlling matriarch, trying to surgically remove a "*hideous story*" from her own brain (243). For instance, the page with the first existing entry, which dates to August 1931, is numbered by Edwina as page "30"; nothing is known about what happened in or to the previous twenty-nine pages. Page 31 ends midsentence, pages 32 through 36 are missing, and the next seven surviving pages are numbered 37 through 43. The remaining pages (into June 1934) are unnumbered. We do not know what entries are missing throughout and thereafter.[6] Given her habit of saving nearly every scrap of writing relating to her beloved son Tom, from school report cards to clippings in the papers about his literary awards, the diary was more than likely left partly intact and simply misplaced among the papers that Andreas Brown, the owner of Gotham Book Mart and Williams's official bibliographer in the early 1960s, eventually discovered in her basement, when he went looking there for important documents that Williams knew she had kept. Dakin Williams eventually procured the collection of entries, before lending it to Leverich, who reproduced parts of it (not always in chronological order) here and there in his 1995 biography of Williams. Leverich informs us, "Edwina kept a diary of this time [1931], discovered many years later among her letters and memorabilia," adding in a brief note that "[t]he diary was found in the Dakin Williams collection" (120).

A group of Dakin's materials (not including the diary) was purchased at a Sotheby's auction on 4 December 1996 by the Rare Book and Manuscript Library of Columbia University.[7] Eventually, the diary was sold to the collector Fred W. Todd, purchased through Brown at the Gotham Book Mart. The Historic New Orleans Collection acquired the diary from Todd in 2002, and it now resides permanently among THNOC's Fred W. Todd Tennessee Williams Collection of manuscripts, letters, memorabilia, and realia.

The entries appear in general to have been written in haste (e.g., Edwina's handwriting is filled with partially crossed *t*'s and periods that extend into dashes) and partly from memory, given the months that separate an event from its recording. Consequently, readers will encounter Edwina's frequent indifference to precise dates, her idiosyncratic spellings, and her quirky punctuation that seems at times like verse scansion, each of which raised several concerns during the diary's editing. For example, the short dashes she scatters throughout read like pauses in thought more than connectors: they are represented here as European-style dashes (short, with a space on either end), whose open appearance conveys her expansive, emotional tone better than standard US dashes (which are long and closed up on both ends). As far as possible, I retained her writing style, though because this transcription is not a critical textual edition but designed for a general readership, some small errors that did not convey voice, era, or meaning have been silently corrected. For instance, older spelling forms for words like "to-day" or "my-self" were retained to preserve the historical moment in which she was writing, whereas obvious misspellings like "corduroi" or "Barramore" were corrected. Grammar or syntactical errors in some of her sentences (such as fragments or run-ons) were kept so as to preserve her voice, but errors such as "its" for "it's" were corrected. Those words that Edwina underscored (whether at the time or on a later rereading) appear here in italics. Her unorthodox method of capitalizing certain nouns but not others was also respected throughout. And finally, all her dates were maintained, but correct years were added in brackets to simplify the reading. For instance, one entry is dated Sunday, 29 August, but a quick search among the calendars offers only two possible years with this day-and-date combination: 1925 and 1937. The first year is obviously too early, and the latter too late. The actual year was almost certainly 1931, when the majority of the diary was written.

Readers of the original pages will also notice that she wrote most of the diary in lead pencil but changed to blue ink for a few entries. While that switch is not in itself revelatory—rare is the person who uses the same writing instrument for four years straight—what is of note is that, just as her son would do later with his own "writer's journal" (*Notebooks* 3) that he kept from 1936 to 1958, Edwina obviously later reread her entries and added additional comments in blue ink to the original text. Be it a few telling words underscored (with two short lines) for emphasis, a phrase entirely crossed out, a note about her embarrassment over a particular event, or a quotation to bring the diary to its close, each of these meta-commentaries demonstrates that Edwina, in this diary, was fully conscious of her role as author chronicling the abuses, physical and psychological, meted out by her husband. (In this publication, these blue-pen changes are printed in gray, in a sans serif typeface.)

2019

As noted above, Leverich's biography contains several passages from this diary, scattered across chapters according to the relevance of their content to Williams's life. The *Review*'s editors felt there was value in reproducing the diary in its entirety, as Edwina herself assembled and organized it, and in letting the accumulation of events and voice speak together as a single entity, curated by its author for her own purposes, not for its relevance to her son. Readers may form their own impressions of Edwina and the voice that appears throughout—a voice in which it is nearly impossible today not to hear echoes of *Glass Menagerie*'s Amanda Wingfield. Robert Bray makes that inevitable comparison between the at-times highly dramatic voice in the diary and Amanda's similarly exaggerated voice in his cleverly titled essay "Edwina Williams's Diary: Through a Glass Menagerie Darkly," written for *The Historic New Orleans Collection Quarterly* just after the diary was acquired. In the piece, Bray rightly separates the two voices and argues for a reading of the diary that "offers the most complete and intimate glimpse yet into the domestic hell of the Williams household": "Edwina, not the most faithful of diarists, would sometimes write every day for a week, then skip several months before making another entry. Nevertheless, the cumulative effect of these lonely jottings is both illuminating and disturbing" (8).

Edwina is not Amanda, at least not entirely, and the Edwina of these diary entries is not the Edwina who later spun her yarns to Lucy Freeman in *Remember Me to Tom*. This is 1931, and that was 1962. The thirty-year interim had obviously changed Edwina, as had the money and eventual independence she obtained when her son signed over to her half of his royalty earnings from *The Glass Menagerie*. She is more confident—defiant, even—in the published memoir, even if the details in it only hint at those in the diary. She was living the experience when she wrote the diary, and she had no assurance that she would ever be freed from C.C.'s financial grip, let alone wealthy in her own right. If anything, she is much more Amanda the heightened drama queen in her memoir than she is here in the diary. For instance, in the diary she writes plainly about having to "g[e]t up as usual at six-thirty to get Cornelius' breakfast," whereas in the memoir she dramatically "drags" herself out of bed to cook for him because it is her wifely duty:

> Many were the times I dragged myself out of bed to fix dinner, for I believed that even though feelings were strained between my husband and myself, I should cook for him, although he would have preferred a thick steak every night to the menus I so frugally planned. In spite of the pain [from a recent surgery], I made a point of being cheerful, for no man wants to come home to a sick and complaining wife. (44–45)

Later, concerning the aftermath of the fight that led to her broken nose, Edwina expresses herself collectedly in her diary: "I went quietly back to the sun-room and gave Cornelius his grip and told him I was tired of these scenes and he could go when-ever he was ready." In her memoir, the more dramatic Edwina reappears:

> Rose was the one who saw my husband abuse me and she lived in fear of him herself. At first his abuse was only verbal. He would regularly order me out of the house once a month, enraged by some trivial occurrence, although I think he would have been astonished had I left. On the one hand he would insist I go, on the other he would snarl, "You needn't try to leave me, because I'll give away every cent I have rather than pay you alimony."
>
> Once I asked him, "Why do you threaten me so, Cornelius?"
>
> "Because I'm unhappy with you," he said.
>
> "There's no point in your being unhappy here. Why don't you just pack your things and go to a hotel? I'll help you," I offered.
>
> He threw some clothes into a valise and stalked out of the house. Rose burst into tears and sobbed on my shoulder, "Mother, he won't ever come back. What will we do?"
>
> I wondered, too. If he left for good, how would I take care of the children? I was not fitted for any kind of work. My parents had no money to speak of. (56)

While it is fruitless to argue which version is more "true," it is important to acknowledge that the narrative in the memoir is mediated—by Freeman, by the passage of time, by its being a conscious performance for a national audience, among other things—even if it is impossible to know what the effects of those mediations are.

Where the memoir is perhaps more valuable than the diary is in the hindsight that Edwina brings to the accounts of her marriage troubles and

C.C.'s alcoholism. Still not entirely willing, either in the diary or in the memoir, to look closely at any role she might have played in the household's tension (not that her choices in any way justify C.C.'s physical and emotional abuse—a fact about which she is admirably clear, more so than many people, then and now), Edwina does try to understand C.C.:

> Cornelius drank so much, I believe, because he was unhappy, not with me, but with his life in general. I am not so egotistical as to think I drove him to drink, for no one is powerful enough to force someone else to do anything he does not wish to do. We know, today, that the roots of such extreme behavior as alcoholism lie deep in an unhappy childhood. (59)

Edwina's reductive but not unsympathetic assessment is typical of pop psychology at the time, evidenced in the many early explanations of the "mystery" of another alcoholic Williams figure, Brick Pollitt. Unlike Brick, though, C.C. (who was already dead by the time Edwina published her memoir) could not supply his own version of his path to alcoholism.

Throughout the years, we have had Tennessee Williams's perspective on his family's battle royal, and here we have Edwina's. It would have been interesting to have C.C.'s too, and in fact Williams himself tries to supply a version of it in his 1960 essay "The Man in the Overstuffed Chair," an encomium of sorts to the abusive and (Williams felt) abused father who rejects his family and wife because they had rejected him: "Cornelius Coffin Williams, the Mississippi drummer, who was removed from the wild and free road and put behind a desk like a jungle animal put in a cage in a zoo" (*New Selected Essays* 99).[8] Like Blanche and Stanley's violent "date with each other from the beginning" (*Streetcar* 402), Edwina and C.C.'s war, according to Williams, emanated from a "tragedy of misunderstandings and insensitivity to others" (*Selected Letters* 2: 118). Bray nods to Williams's viewpoint in conceding that specifics about who contributed what to the "marital acrimony [. . .] can only be the subject of speculation, even by her children, for Cornelius apparently never documented his side of the relationship." But he also affirms, "There can be no doubt about her suffering" (9).

Given the various and, at times, conflicting portraits of Edwina that have been provided over the years—through her portrayal as Amanda, through Williams's descriptions of her elsewhere in his writing, and through her own memoir about her famous son—it is tempting to read these diary entries, as both Leverich and Bray have suggested, as further evidence of Edwina's self-dramatization. Rather than spend time fruitlessly speculating about whether Edwina, like Blanche, is reporting what *ought* to be the truth, it is more prudent to go back to *Suddenly Last Summer*, where a powerful matriarch and a distraught victim fight for control of the trauma narrative, and take heed of Dr. Cukrowicz's response to Violet Venable's command that he "*cut this hideous story out*" of Catharine's brain: "we ought at least to consider the possibility that the girl's story could be true" (423). Even better, we should assume Edwina's report in the diary is true—is, at the very least, *a* truth—and proceed accordingly.

Notes

I thank my UE 703 graduate students at the Université de Lorraine for their help in preparing this manuscript for publication.

[1] Leverich 109, 134. On the history of the role played by propriety in divorce in the US South, see Censer.

[2] It should be noted that, in the United States, "cruelty, desertion, or nonsupport were more common justifications for granting women divorce decrees than was adultery" (Block 162), and C.C. was surely guilty of all four. See Salmon.

[3] For more on the public use of a woman's private diary in a London divorce court in 1858, see Summerscale.

[4] See, for instance, Williams's *Memoirs* (25–39) and Dakin Williams and Shepherd Mead's *Tennessee Williams: An Intimate Biography* (31–45). In a letter to Rose, dated 5 December 1931, Williams expresses his frightful anticipation on returning home for the Christmas holidays: "As you can readily understand, I am very anxious to hear from you concerning the situation on the home front. Has the spirit of Quiet Night now descended?" (*Selected Letters* 1: 57).

[5] Edwina, for instance, complains in one entry about having been ordered by C.C. to fire the maid, who did all the family cleaning and the laundry. It was the height of the Depression, after all, but Edwina is still trying to maintain her southern bourgeois lifestyle and climb the St. Louis social ladder through all of their removals to more affluent neighborhoods—all while men in middle management, as C.C. was, were losing their jobs.

[6] Her lack of attention to pagination is a trait she passed on to her son, whose college teachers would repeatedly scold him for it in his essays.

[7] Columbia University notes of the provenance of its Tennessee Williams Papers that "The largest part of the present collection was purchased from the Tennessee Williams estate in 1994 and consists primarily of material found in the Key West

house." It adds the following to this larger acquisition: "Shortly thereafter, a small collection of family letters dating from Williams' early life was purchased from his brother Dakin through Sotheby's" (Smith and Cannan).

[8] "The Man in the Overstuffed Chair" is set largely in 1943 and after, although Williams does recall earlier times at home in St. Louis. While not entirely redemptive of his father, the essay is more sympathetic and tries to negotiate Williams's "curiously mixed feelings of disgust and pity" for his father (*New Selected Essays* 99), probably because he had recently passed away at the time of its writing and because Williams had now himself lived in at least two long-term and troubled relationships. In fact, Williams speaks more in this essay about his time working alongside his father at Continental than he does in his *Memoirs*.

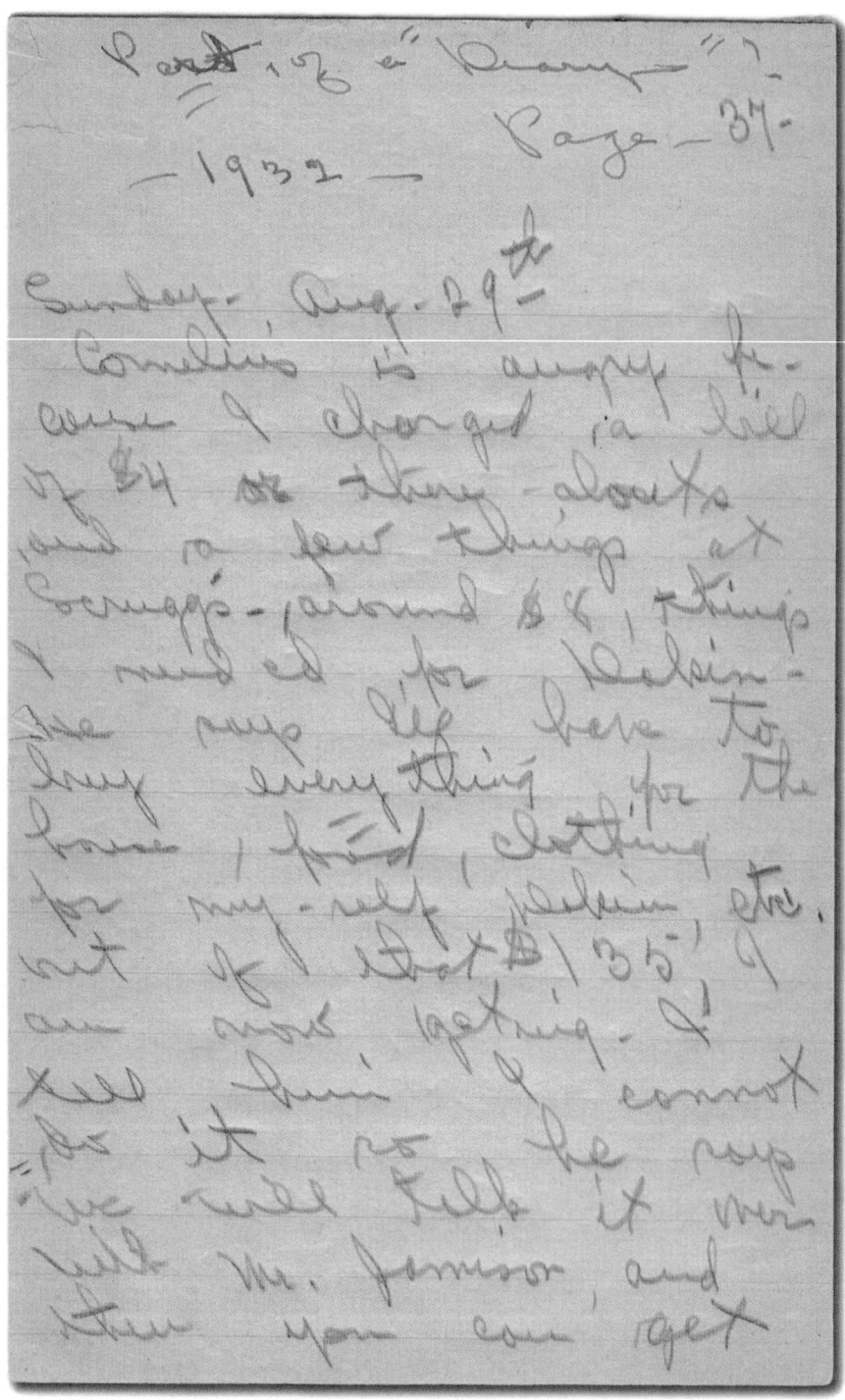

Page from a diary entry by Edwina Dakin Williams, mother of Tennessee Williams. The Fred W. Todd Tennessee Williams Collection at The Historic New Orleans Collection, 2002-79-L.2; MSS 562.25.4.

Diary Entries, 1931 to 1934
Edwina Dakin Williams

Printed by permission of the Dakin Williams Estate.

Mother[1] (as always) comes to the rescue. When I leave the Hospital (at the end of three days during which they examine my kidneys) I have to go for treatments every day for about three weeks.[2] Dr. Carroll[3] asks me if my husband is not un-easy about me! I have never known him to be!

Aug. 16th [1931]

Cornelius takes away the ten dollars, leaving me the one hundred and the pension check of thirty-five. His salary has been reduced fifty dollars, he tells me. I'm needing some things for the house but he says I cannot get them now. We have not enough sheets, napkins are in rags, but I will wait until next month and try my luck again. While Mother was here I took a three day trip on the river to Keokuk dam, my

---

[1] The entry with the earliest date appears on a manuscript page numbered by Edwina as page 30. Pages 1–29 of the diary are missing.

[2] Edwina notes in *Remember Me to Tom* that she was frequently ill from 1925 onward, and that Grand, her mother, often came up from Clarksdale or Memphis to take care of the household while she was in the hospital or recuperating at home: "I was ill during most of Tom's high school days, first undergoing five minor operations and then a major one. [. . .] Mother would always help out when needed. Rose would telephone and plead, 'Grand, come quick. Mother's sick,' and her grandmother would board the next train for St. Louis" (44).

[3] Possibly Dr. Henry Relton McCarroll, intern in surgery (1931–32) and assistant resident surgeon (1932–33) at Barnes Hospital in St. Louis.

"vacation."[4] It only cost sixteen dollars something, which I pay from the birth-day gifts of father and mother. Cornelius gave me – nothing, but[5]

Part of a "Diary"?[6]

Page – 37

– 193[1] –[7]

Sunday – Aug. 29th [1931][8]

Cornelius is angry because I charged a bill of $4 or there-abouts and a few things at Scruggs[9] – around $8, things I needed for Dakin. He

---

[4] "Keokuk dam" refers to US Lock and Dam No. 19. The dam, an engineering marvel completed in 1913 (the main locks were added in the 1950s), is located on the upper Mississippi River near Keokuk, Iowa, roughly 180 miles from St. Louis.

[5] The text cuts off here. These first two entries appear on pages Edwina numbered 30 and 31. The next page in the sequence is numbered 37.

[6] Throughout this publication, gray text in a sans serif typeface indicates a place where Edwina used blue pen to add marks to the original pencil entries. Just as her son Tom would do in his own writer's journal, Edwina reread her diary at a later date and added metacommentary, made deletions, underscored words, and made other changes.

[7] Here, Edwina wrote the words "*Part* of a 'Diary'?" at the top of the page, added the year (which looks like 1932, though context suggests the original entry was in fact written in 1931) and wrote the word "page" next to the original (pencil) page number (see image on p. 18). Leverich places the original diary entry, which he cites in full, in 1932 (134). Given that this entry is followed by other entries dated in September, of which one has Williams going off to college on Wednesday, 9 September, it is more probable that the year is 1931.

[8] Edwina appears to have gotten either the day or the date wrong when writing the original entry. The only years around this time when 29 August fell on a Sunday were 1926 and 1937, the first too early and the second too late, per the other entries.

[9] One of St. Louis's three main department stores (the other two were Famous-Barr and Stix, Baer, and Fuller), Scruggs-Vandervoort-Barney was located downtown at 915 Olive Street in the former Syndicate Trust and Century buildings. Founded in 1850 as a dry goods store, it closed in 1967. Scruggs-Vandervoort-Barney celebrated the grand opening celebration on 21 September 1951 of a branch store on Hanley Road and Forsyth Boulevard in Clayton, Missouri, where the Williamses had lived, but Edwina's letter predates this branch by nearly twenty years, so she is talking about the downtown store here.

says I'll have to buy *every*thing for the house, food, clothing for my-self, Dakin, etc. out of that $135, I am now getting. I tell him I cannot do it so he says "We will talk it over with Mr. Jamison,[10] and then you can get out." Alright, I've done the best I could. My conscience is clear. My poor little children. What will become of them. I've had such a struggle trying to build strong bodies for them with ~~the poor misfortune that is theirs.~~[11] My knees and hands are trembling so I cannot write more – What-ever comes God is my strength and my refuge.

Aug. 30th [1931]

After telling me he intended to divorce me (on what grounds!?), C. put on his hat and left the house. I told him to do as he pleased. Of course he has no grounds as he well knows. Of course he is just trying to make things so un-bearable for me that I'll have to leave, but I cannot desert these children.

Sep. 1st [1931]

Nothing more is said. Things go on as usual. I do not know if he has stopped charge accounts at the Dry-Goods stores[12] as he has threatened. Such a hectic time as I've had all these years to get the necessities for these children. Many times they would have suffered had it not been for the help I've received from mother and father.

I am thankful, though, that Cornelius now gives Rose a regular allowance with which to clothe her-self, thirty dollars a month after the dental work is deducted. She wants to have some bridge-work done

---

[10] Paul Jamison was Cornelius's (C.C.'s) boss and Edwina's "confidant and close personal friend" (Leverich 134). According to Leverich, Jamison and Edwina flirted a lot, so much so that they became a subject of local gossip: Leverich writes that Edwina's mother overheard two women discussing their "affair" in a department store and scolded her daughter (109).

[11] This passage is crossed out in blue ink, suggesting that Edwina deleted it not immediately but at a later date.

[12] Perhaps Scruggs and Famous-Barr.

now. The vacant spaces do look badly in a young girl's mouth.[13] I had to let mother take the ring Mrs. Mead gave her home with her to keep her from selling it. Father wrote her that he would buy it (of course he will give it back to her) and to-day he sent her a check for fifty dollars as a first payment. He needs everything he has, I'm afraid, now that he has retired.[14] And I hated to have him do it, but she would have sold it to some one else. She and I went to a jeweler to have it valued before Mother took it away. He valued it at $150.

Sep. 4th 1931. (Very embarrassing)

I receive notice through the mail that our charge accounts at the Dry Goods stores have been discontinued.

Sat. Sep. 5th [1931]

I took Tom to town to buy his shirts, socks etc. as he leaves for College next Wednesday.[15] We bought most of his things in Boyd's[16] basement to get them as cheaply as possible, had them sent C.O.D.

In the after-noon I did my marketing, carrying everything home as I now have no charge account at the Grocery stores. Cornelius generally

---

[13] Rose had had problems with her teeth, noting in a letter to her mother dated February 1938 that "I have to go to the dentist, have lost several fillings" (qtd. in Leverich 252).

[14] Walter E. Dakin, Williams's grandfather, retired in April 1931 (T. Williams, *Selected Letters* 1: 56). Leverich dates the retirement earlier: "In January 1931, [Dakin] had retired [. . .] and began moving out of the rectory" (120).

[15] Williams was entering his third year at the University of Missouri at Columbia, leaving on Wednesday, 9 September 1931. Leverich notes that "Tom was anxious to get back to Columbia, not only to get free of his job [as a typist at Continental Shoe] but also to get away from his parents, whose battles were now at their worst" (120).

[16] Founded in 1876 by Trustin B. Boyd, Boyd's Department Store was located at 6th and Olive Streets in downtown St. Louis. The establishment built its reputation on specialty and custom clothing and accessories for men, eventually evolving into one of the most popular stores among downtown shoppers. Like many department stores, Boyd's had a bargain basement (known as Boyd's Subway), where cheaper "end of series" items could be found. Like Scruggs, Boyd's opened a branch in Clayton, but not until the 1950s.

comes home late for his supper on Sat. evenings as he goes out to a country club on that after-noon ostensibly for golf, but mainly for drinking. For supper I made some Chili-con-carne of which he is very fond and it is something that can easily be kept hot. Tom and Rose leave early for a card party. Cornelius does not show up for supper, or even telephone. I wait up for the children. They come in at 2 o'clock, Cornelius not 'til 3 o'clock, stayed for the dinner-dance at the club.[17] He becomes angry because I reproached him for not letting me know he would not be home for supper. He has had too much to drink, tells me in a voice loud enough to wake the neighbor-hood that I make "life a hell" for him, and can leave.[18]

Oct. [1931]

Cornelius leaves on a ten day business trip. I'm wondering how I'll make the twenty dollars I now have on hand feed us, pay for laundry and car-fare etc. I had to have a suit cleaned for Dakin and Rose's comfort[er], also Dakin's corduroy coat, amounting to $3.00.

Nov. 9th 1931[19]

We've had two terrible scenes since Cornelius' return. In both of them he says he is going to "quit" me. A nice sense of security that gives to the children. No wonder they are both nervous. I receive a letter from the school doctor saying Dakin is "nineteen pounds under-weight" and I've been trying so hard to build him up giving him hot malted milk every night etc.

---

[17] C.C. was a member of Westborough Country Club in Webster Groves, where Williams would occasionally swim (E. Williams, *Remember* 68; Leverich 144). A 19 June 1934 letter from Williams to his grandfather reports that Williams would drive Rose, Dakin, and himself to the club during the summer evenings in his new, secondhand roadster, which he called "Scatterbolt," to swim, play tennis, and golf (*Selected Letters* 1: 28, 71–72, 72n).

[18] The editors of the *Selected Letters* note that C.C. and Edwina were "openly and bitterly divided at this time" (1: 58n).

[19] Edwina reread this entry and underlined the year, 1931, twice in blue pen. She added the same double underline to two words—"awakened" and "gay"— that appear later in the entry (see note 21, below).

Cornelius has reduced Rose's allowance to twenty-five a month.

I had to hand him a bill that has come to the house for several months yester-day morning. It was from Barnes hospital for the "Shadow pictures" Dr. Alexander[20] had made of Rose last spring. This occasioned an-other tempest and when I very mildly reminded him it wasn't my fault or Rose's either – He interpreted me as giving him a "dirty crack" and said, "one more and I leave you"! While he was away Dakin needed a pair of corduroy trousers for school wear and as the charge accounts had been stopped at the other stores, I charged it at Scruggs. He said "I will stop that, too, and furthermore you'll have to pay that bill your-self"! We ended the argument by his having to take the bills away with him but I'm wondering how much longer I can endure this. I had *awakened* feeling so

---

[20] Leverich notes that a certain Dr. Alexander was the "family physician," and, in 1934, Rose began seeing a psychiatrist at Barnes Hospital, who diagnosed her physical ailments, especially her stomach issues, as "a lack of self-confidence" and "a fear of sex, stemming from her mother's own puritanical abhorrence" (141). The first of these two doctors was probably Harry Louis Alexander, MD, associate professor of medicine at Washington University and associate physician at Barnes Hospital in 1931 (*Bulletin* [1931] 8, 35, 41, 43). In a letter dated 16 June 1930, Williams wrote to his grandfather that "Rose's clinical examinations at Barnes' proved that her trouble was solely nervous. She is now under the care of a nerve specialist" (*Selected Letters* 1: 52). Correcting brother Tom's claim that it was "old Doc Alexander" who had diagnosed Rose's problem in 1935 as sexual regression and prescribed that she find a lover (T. Williams, *Memoirs* 119; cf. E. Williams, *Remember Me to Tom* 58), Dakin Williams writes that the second doctor, the psychiatrist, was actually "Dr. Beckman" (Williams and Mead 36). The *Bulletin of Washington University* for 1931 lists a J. William Beckmann, MD, as "Assistant Neurologist to Barnes Hospital" (28) and "Instructor in Clinical Neurology" (95), so it is probable that this Dr. Beckmann was Rose's psychiatrist at Barnes. Margaret Bradham Thornton cites a letter from Edwina to her parents written in January 1937, where Edwina mentions that Rose was being treated by "Dr. Alexander" and "Dr. Saterfield" (T. Williams, *Notebooks* 72n115). The *Bulletin of Washington University* for 1936 lists Val Beyer Satterfield, MD, as an instructor at Washington University who taught the course Neurological Clinic: "The diagnosis and treatment of neuroses from the standpoint of psycho-biology. Case material and clinic patients are used for purposes of discussion" (*Bulletin* [1936] 62). The doctor's first name may well have stuck with Williams, who would begin writing about Val Xavier in *Battle of Angels* a few years later.

gay.[21] It was a beautiful morning, the sun shining brightly, and though I was tired from the strenuous Sunday (We motored to Columbia the day before and had a nice visit with Tom at the fraternity house[22]), I got up as usual at six-thirty to get Cornelius' breakfast and was happy in thinking how well Tom looked and to find that he had been doing well in his journalistic work. *Then* – the thunder-bolt! I was perfectly calm until he left, and then I was so weak I could scarcely get Dakin's breakfast and get him off to school. I also had to dress and go to Erker's[23] to have Tom's glasses mended (I found he was using them tied to-gether with a piece of string). He said he had them mended once in Columbia but they had broken again immediately. If I had mentioned it to Cornelius there would have been another racket, so I took them down and paid for them myself. So many things like that come up that I pay for out of my allowance and say nothing about it.

I must stop to get the dinner. I've had to let Laura, the maid go as Cornelius says I must find a cheaper one. She is the first one I've had since I came to St. Louis who could get a meal on the table with-out

---

[21] The words "awakened" and "gay" are underscored twice in blue pen, obviously at a later date. Since Edwina writes her 27 June 1932 entry in the same blue pen, it is probable that, on that date, she read the earlier entries up to December 1931 (where she had left off), underscored the two words, and then resumed writing the diary with the June 1932 entry. While in the 1930s the word *gay* was not yet widely associated with homosexuality among the general (straight) population, the usage was on the rise: it is possible that Edwina underscored these two words because, in hindsight, she now understood their meanings—and their relation to her son—in a different light.

[22] During his first semester, in 1929, Williams had joined the Alpha Tau Omega fraternity, ascribable to some degree to his father's intervention (he had not attended rush week [*Selected Letters* 1: 31n]). C.C., who had been a member of Pi Kappa Alpha at the University of Tennessee, thought the fraternity would help "make a man out of his son" (Leverich 108). Williams had moved into the fraternity's newly built house in January 1930 (Leverich 109; *Selected Letters* 1: 39, 41).

[23] Established in 1879, Erker's Fine Eyewear still (as of this writing) maintains a shop at 908 Olive Street in downtown St. Louis, just across from the former Scruggs department store. Erker's developed the goggles Charles Lindbergh had used on his solo transatlantic flight from New York to France.

assistance from me, so I give her up with regrets! Scruggs call up to know if it's "authentic" that the charge account there has been discontinued![24]

Nov. 29th 1931 –

Quite the biggest up-heaval we've had yet was staged to-day – Sunday. It was the new girl's pay-day and Cornelius became infuriated because I had not obtained her cheaper. She is to do the laundry and cleaning. I've been doing all the cooking for the past few weeks. Also I had run out of money and couldn't pay for the shoes I bought at the office yesterday and for which he had to advance the money $2.60, I believe. Such a torrent of abuse as he heaped upon me! The children were present and he said "I'm leaving you. I'll pack my grip and go to the hotel." Both Dakin and Rose became hysterical.[25] Cornelius then turned on Rose berating her for everything imaginable. "Dakin is the only one

---

[24] C.C.'s practice of canceling the family's charge accounts without warning is noted by Dakin Williams as well: Dakin recalls that the Famous-Barr department store called Edwina up just after the nose-breaking incident on New Year's Day 1933 (see p. 28, below) to tell her that

> her charge privilege had been canceled, a call that galvanized her like a clarion call of a Civil War bugle boy to action. A call from Miss Edwina and C.C. was called on the carpet by his boss, Paul Jamison. C.C. was ordered to fire his amorous secretary (or be fired himself) and to immediately restore mother's charge account at Famous. (Williams and Mead 36)

C.C. used money as a weapon against his wife, who often had to turn to her parents for financial support in helping the children. C.C.'s handling of the family finances was a bone of contention between the couple, a problem exacerbated by the Depression and the toll it was taking among St. Louis's middle class. As Leverich writes, "The truth was, Cornelius did not cut corners when it came to his own pleasures, and he continued to indulge in country club golf and weekend binges" (125).

[25] Rose began fighting more frequently with C.C. from 1930 onward. As Williams wrote to his grandfather in June 1930, Rose "had a quarrel with Dad last night and became so furious that she left the house and spent the night with Miss Florence who happened to be visiting us. She declares that she will never come back. However, I think she will change her mind. Her trouble is certainly a great worry to Mother and Grand and myself but I think the doctor will be able to get her out of it" (*Selected Letters* 1: 52).

of you worth a d—" said he, as he flung him-self out of the room. Tom was packing his grip in his little room preparing to leave for Columbia on the two o'clock train. "Mother," said he, "tell him to get the h— out of here" the first time I've ever heard Tom be profane. I went quietly back to the sun-room and gave Cornelius his grip and told him I was tired of these scenes and he could go when-ever he was ready, that I couldn't have Dakin made a nervous wreck as he has made Rose. He announced he would go when he got ready.

Next day.

Tom stayed until the mid-night train as he didn't want to leave me with such a storm brewing. Cornelius has calmed down and evidently decided to remain. Poor Rose was ill all night and couldn't sleep. I feel as weak as if I'd gotten up from a sick-bed. How much longer can I endure this? Tom said, as far as he was concerned, he'd rather go to work and live in the cheapest part of the city than see me go through this any more.

Dec. 1st [1931]

We will have a few days of peace and quiet. Cornelius is leaving for Chicago on a short business trip.

June 27th 1932 – [26]

Things have been moving along very harmoniously as I do not ask anything of Cornelius and what I cannot buy out of my allowance I do with-out. We really hear less about our "poverty" than we did during all those years the rest of the world were enjoying their prosperity. With the

---

[26] This entry is written in blue ink, suggesting it was added just after Edwina had read the previous entries of her diary, up to the 1 December 1931 entry (see note 21, above). Williams, who had worked at the Continental branch of the International Shoe Company the previous summer to help pay for his third year of college, was back working there again, now full-time since his father had refused his returning to Mizzou in the fall to finish his studies. For nearly three years, until 1935, Williams worked as a clerk-typist and lived his "season in hell" here and in his parents' home, as he describes it in his 1941 essay "Random Observations," used as a preface to his play *Stairs to the Roof* (xxi).

exception of one evening about three weeks ago when Cornelius said he was going to have to take Tom out of school and that Rose would have to "clerk," things have been quite peaceful. Rose cried all the next day because she still is not well.[27]

New Year's Day – 1933 –

Will be long remembered by the children and me. Cornelius stayed out all night, came home at seven while I was preparing break-fast. I made the mistake of protesting, not realizing how much under the influence of liquor he was. I asked him to go to bed in Tom's room as Dakin was asleep in mine. He flew into a rage and threatened me. I locked my door and tried to reason with him through the closed door. "Open that door or I'll bust it in!" Before I could obey the command he had suited the action to the word, the lock broke, the door flew open striking me in the nose and knocking me to the floor where I lay dazed. In the meanwhile, Rose wakens, hears the commotion, sees me lying on the floor with nose bleeding and rushes into the hall [of the apartment building] screaming "Help, he is killing her." I come to my senses, find Cornelius bending over me and a strange man in the hall, had a nervous chill – the children send for a doctor.[28]

---

[27] The text ends here, at the bottom of the page, and the next entry—dated New Year's Day, 1933—begins at the top of a new page, so it is difficult to ascertain whether Edwina stopped her journal for nearly seven months or if she continued writing onto one or more pages that are now missing. (She had stopped numbering the pages of her journal in November 1931.)

[28] In *Remember Me to Tom*, Edwina recalls this event thus:

> Cornelius really started to frighten me, however, when he became very drunk and was not himself. One night, after he obviously had been drinking, he walked into the bathroom where I was standing and threatened angrily, "I'm going to kill you!"
> I fled in terror in to my bedroom and quickly locked the door. He pounded on it as he kept shouting, "Come out of there. I'm going to kill you!" He was almost six feet tall and very stocky, almost fat from all the drinking, and he broke down the door. It struck me and I fainted, mostly from fear.
> Rose witnessed this fight and others. (57)

Leverich writes that in the New Year 1933, while "the entire nation was looking hopefully to the new president," there was "no celebration on the family

July 26th 1933 – [29]

By being extremely tactful and asking nothing of Cornelius I have managed to keep the home fairly peaceful. There have been only two major up-heavals. One, about a week before New Year's day when Cornelius remained out all night. I made the mistake of reproaching him immediately instead of waiting until he had slept off the effect of the liquor he had been drinking all night. When he passed me on the way to the bath-room, he said "When I come out, I'm going to knock you down." This frightened me, and I locked my door. The lock did not hold and he burst in the door with me behind it knocking me un-conscious. When I regained my senses, I heard Rose screaming and a strange man's voice in the hall, and Cornelius telling him to go away, that I was alright. I'll not write more except to say I was sick after-ward and the children sent for Dr. Falk.[30]

Sometime in June, I think it was, I told Cornelius we were out of sheets and I would have to buy some. This was the occasion of a terrible out-burst, said he didn't have the money, that he was going to stop my

---

battlefront, however: the marriage of Edwina and Cornelius Williams had hit rock bottom" (137–38). Leverich's description of the altercation—which left Edwina with a broken nose—is not particularly sympathetic: he quotes Amanda Wingfield, opining that the injury allowed Edwina to assume the role of "a Christian martyr." The incident forced the marriage to a crisis point, and, as Leverich sees it, "[g]radually, very gradually, the dominant roles were reversed, until finally C.C.'s threats and roars became meaningless echoes" (139).

[29] As this entry begins on a new page, and the previous entry had space left on the page to write on, it is possible that Edwina had forgotten over the course of the six interim months that she had already recounted the broken-down door story. There is no way to know whether she wrote other (now missing) entries during that time.

[30] Probably Dr. Oswald P. J. Falk, a diagnostician, whose offices in the University Club Tower in Richmond Heights were only a few miles from the 6254 Enright Avenue apartment in University City, a middle-class suburb in western St. Louis. The Harry Ransom Humanities Research Center at the University of Texas, Austin, holds a 4 June 1935 invoice issued by "Dr. O. P. J. Falk" to "Tom Williams," for services that include "[t]wo house calls and office visit" (box 57, folder 10). It is also worth noting that, while the gist of the story remains intact in the three versions she recounts, the details are notably different.

allowance (his pension check of $35, as the government were going to discontinue them) and that Tom would have to begin to pay board. He made Tom leave the University and go to work on a small salary in the Vitality branch of the International Shoe Co.[31] and it has taken all of his salary to pay for the accident he had last summer[32] and his clothing, lunch money, etc. He would have received his degree in Journalism this Spring which is the kind of work he loves to do.[33]

This morning he flew into a rage because I was getting two quarts of milk daily again! Dakin has a bad boil on his leg and is needing to drink more milk. Rose hasn't been so well again and I want her to have a cup of hot milk before retiring. He said I was spending too much on food and that *he* was going to buy it here-after, and take the food allowance out of my hands. There was a case of "Schlitz" beer under the kitchen table and I suggested it might be well to economize on that instead of the children's milk. That didn't help matters. I suppose I should have kept quiet.

Aug. 5th – 1933

Twice this month Cornelius has remained out all night.[34]

---

[31] C.C. withdrew his son from the University of Missouri in the summer of 1932 because of his failing grades and forced him to work as a clerk-typist in the Continental branch of the International Shoe Company for a salary of $65 a month.

[32] In August 1932, Williams had an accident at the Westborough Country Club swimming pool where he knocked out his front teeth. In a letter to his fraternity brother, dated 19 August 1932, Williams writes that he has been "laid up the past few weeks with a crack[ed] upper jaw and a number of semi-detached molars" (*Selected Letters* 1: 63). In *Remember Me to Tom*, Edwina describes the accident in these terms: "One day I was sitting in the garden, enjoying one of my rare moments of peace in St. Louis, when I looked up to see Tom stagger out of a car, handkerchief held to his mouth. As he took the handkerchief away, I nearly fainted. His mouth was one bloody mess. [. . .] Tom had walked out on the diving board at the club, jumped, and crashed into the edge of the cement pool. He knocked two front teeth out of his mouth and chipped off others" (68; cf. Leverich 128, 131).

[33] Leverich cites the last two sentences from this entry (128), noting that they come from the diary but misidentifying the source as Edwina's *Remember Me to Tom* in his endnote.

[34] Leverich cites this entry in full, adding: "On August 5, Edwina Williams made a brief entry in her diary. [. . .] After that, she would have less and less to

Jan. 1934.

Managed to get along with the minimum of friction. Cornelius made a terrible scene New Year's Eve because he said we had used all the gasoline in the car the evening before. (We rarely use the car.) He took the car, went off returning about one-thirty. We went to Church on the street-car.

June – 15th – 1934

Cornelius flew into an insane rage yesterday evening because I had charged a pair of white pants for Dakin – said he would stop our charge accounts again!

No more this time. Not because "there isn't any more."

Quote from
Ethel Barrymore[35]

---

add before she tucked the tiny notebook away, later believing she had destroyed it (139–40).

[35] This last sentence, written in blue ink, was apparently added sometime later, when Edwina felt she needed to conclude the entries. "That's all there is, there isn't any more" is a line from the play *Sunday*, written by three English actors—Horace Hodges, Edward Irwin, and T. Wigney Percyval—under the nom de plume Thomas Raceward. Ethel Barrymore starred in Charles Frohman's 1904 production of the play at the Hudson Theatre and, in response to repeated curtain calls from her adoring fans, recited the line, which she had just delivered in the fourth act. The line was later referenced and parodied throughout the 1920s and 1930s in songs and in movies, often changed to "That's all there is, there ain't no more." While the line's popularity was no doubt the reason for choosing it as her final entry, Edwina may also have been (consciously or unconsciously) drawn to Barrymore for more personal reasons: Barrymore's 1923 divorce occasioned reports that the actor herself had been physically abused by her husband, Russell Griswold Colt, who reportedly fathered a child by another woman (*Boston Post* 6 July 1923). See Partridge 453. See also Barrymore.

Works Cited

Barrymore, Ethel. *Memories: An Autobiography*. Hulton Press, 1955.

Block, Sharon. "Lines of Color, Sex and Service: Comparative Sexual Coercion in Early America." *Sex, Love, Race: Crossing Boundaries in North American History*, edited by Martha Hodes, New York UP, 1999, pp. 141–63.

Bray, Robert. "Edwina Williams's Diary: Through a Glass Menagerie Darkly." *The Historic New Orleans Collection Quarterly*, vol. 21, no. 1, Winter 2003, pp. 8–9.

Bulletin of Washington University, Saint Louis: Forty-Second Annual Catalog of the School of Medicine, vol. 29, no. 11, Apr. 1931.

Bulletin of Washington University, Saint Louis: Forty-Seventh Annual Catalog of the School of Medicine, vol. 34, no. 11, Apr. 1936.

Censer, Jane Turner. "'Smiling through Her Tears': Ante-Bellum Southern Women and Divorce." *American Journal of Legal History*, vol. 25, 1981, pp. 24–47.

Leverich, Lyle. *Tom: The Unknown Tennessee Williams*. Hodder and Stoughton, 1995.

Millim, Anne-Marie. *The Victorian Diary: Authorship and Emotional Labour*. 2013. Routledge, 2016.

Partridge, Eric. *A Dictionary of Catch Phrases*. Routledge, 1986.

Salmon, Marylynn. *Women and the Law of Property in Early America*. U of North Carolina P, 1989.

Smith, G., and G. Cannan, preparers. "Tennessee Williams (1911–1983): 1882 (1942) – 1983." Rare Book and Manuscript Library, Columbia U, 4 Feb. 2000, www.columbia.edu/cu/lweb/eresources/archives/rbml/Williams/main.html.

Snell, James. "Marital Cruelty: Women and the Nova Scotia Divorce Court, 1900–1939." *Acadiensis*, vol. 18, no. 1, Autumn 1988, pp. 3–32.

Summerscale, Kate. *Mrs. Robinson's Disgrace: The Private Diary of a Victorian Lady*. Bloomsbury, 2012.

Williams, Dakin, and Shepherd Mead. *Tennessee Williams: An Intimate Biography*. Arbor, 1983.

Williams, Edwina Dakin, and Lucy Freeman. *Remember Me to Tom*. Sunrise, 1963.

Williams, Tennessee. *Memoirs*. 1975. New Directions, 2006.

———. *New Selected Essays: Where I Live*. Edited by John S. Bak, New Directions, 2009.

———. *Notebooks*. Edited by Margaret Bradham Thornton, Yale UP, 2006.

———. *The Selected Letters of Tennessee Williams*. Edited by Albert J. Devlin and Nancy M. Tischler, New Directions, 2000–04. 2 vols.

———. *Stairs to the Roof*. Edited by Allean Hale, New Directions, 2000.

———. *A Streetcar Named Desire*. *The Theatre of Tennessee Williams*, vol. 1, New Directions, 1971, pp. 239–419.

———. *Suddenly Last Summer*. *The Theatre of Tennessee Williams*, vol. 3, New Directions, 1971, pp. 343–423.

"Seuls les Inconnus Pouvaient M'aveugler le Cœur": Reconsidering Cocteau's *Streetcar*

Julie Vatain-Corfdir

A 1971 collection of essays on the reception of *A Streetcar Named Desire* juxtaposes reviews of three national premieres, all penned by seasoned critics. Of Elia Kazan's Broadway staging, Irwin Shaw writes that it is a "magnificent play, magnificently done," praising Tennessee Williams's "triumphantly heightened realism" (45). Of Laurence Olivier's production at the Aldwych, Harold Hobson maintains, amid controversies concerning the decency of the play, that it is "a distinguished work," "noble," and he applauds the "almost unbearably poignant" performance of Vivien Leigh (48). In stark contrast to these discussions of the merits of the work or the acting, the final review in the collection, which turns to the Paris premiere of *Un tramway nommé Désir*—Jean Cocteau's adaptation of *Streetcar*, directed by Raymond Rouleau in 1949[1]—reads as something out of the finer slapstick passages of P. G. Wodehouse. In an unashamedly satirical piece entitled "Laughter dans le Tramway" for the *Atlantic Monthly*, the British critic René MacColl portrays the French production as a "risible piece of entertainment," "almost as uproarious as the Marx Brothers at their topmost peak": he copiously makes fun of the actors unrealistically getting drunk on half a bottle of beer and of the "special off-mauve light" turned on the fine back muscles of Yves Vincent (as Stanley) every time he strips off his shirt, which is frequently (49–50). Thus reads MacColl's account of the last two scenes of *Un tramway nommé Désir*:

> [T]he subtle French prefer to leave nothing to chance. They call in *le symbolisme* to aid *l'amour*. Stan does three mad

entrechats across the stage, wearing a pair of bright red silk pajama trousers, but with bared torso-back strictly audience-wards. Blanche glances up from her dreams of *la plantation*, startled. *"Brute, va!"* she ejaculates. Black-out.

But immediately, through the diaphanous walls, you can perceive, in the street outside, a colored shimmy dancer billowing around to the sound of voodoo drums. The audience is notably entranced by this conceit. *"Ah, ces Américains!"* they observe knowingly to one another. [. . .]

And obviously there's only one remedy. Yes, the Great American Remedy: call in the psychiatrist. [. . .] So, in a surprise ending, Blanche neatly turns the tables on Stan-le-Brute, Meetch-le-Milksop, Stella-la-Femme, the card players, shimmy dancers, and ertderg[2] men. [. . .]

And as she sweeps out in triumph, arm in arm with Monsieur le Directeur du Snake-Pit, all hands burst into tears of jealous rage and maudlin self-pity. (51–52)

It's hard to tell whether MacColl's whimsical prose is aimed more pointedly at Rouleau's choices in staging, at the composition of *Streetcar* itself, or quite simply at French audiences and their stereotypical expectations of American art. While MacColl's may be the most amusing in a string of damning reviews—French and international—of Rouleau's production, it is nonetheless telling that this piece should be chosen for reprinting more than twenty years after the opening of *Streetcar* rather than, for instance, Frank Dorsey's much more positive review of the same production, also readily available in English. Despite a run of well over two hundred performances, despite the high praise bestowed upon the French actors' performances and Cocteau's adaptation, *Un tramway nommé Désir* went down in theatrical memory as a resounding flop, a glaring example of the cultural incompatibilities between France and the United States, so misguided it bordered on comical. Paris did not see another production for decades.

It may be time to qualify, at least in part, such a pessimistic assessment of Rouleau's production. The condescending dismissal of the play by the majority of critics, which has been rightly documented (Falb; Kolin; Savran), may well have obscured some of the more intriguing aesthetic choices jointly made by Cocteau and Rouleau. Scholars have aptly discussed the underlying anti-American sentiment and the feeling of cultural superiority that no doubt colored the Paris reception of the play (Savran) as well as the discrepancies in dramatic aesthetics that made Williams's play appear, to French audiences, at once too old-fashioned and vulgar in its naturalism and too cinematic in its episodic quality (Kolin). Little critical attention, however, has been paid to the language of Cocteau's text itself. To my knowledge, only Gérard Lieber has directly discussed the manuscript, in an essay aimed not at shedding light on *Streetcar* but at defining Cocteau's approach to adaptation, while the recording of a performance, which was made for the Radiodiffusion Française, has so far not been considered. The present essay attempts to define Cocteau and Rouleau's approach more finely by looking closely at the French text and its vocal realization in performance, taking into account the casting and persona of the lead female actor, the (in)famous Arletty. The language, intonation, and pace, as well as the radio commentator's descriptions of the staging, bring into sharper focus the misapprehensions and aesthetic meeting points between *Streetcar* and *Tramway*, along with the intended variations in tone and balance that make Cocteau's adaptation a complex and personal text and revelatory case study for the reception of American drama in France.

Cocteau as Adaptor

Why was Jean Cocteau, who spoke very little English, asked to write the French text of *Streetcar*? And why has his version not been used for other productions, or indeed been reprinted since the original luxurious Bordas edition that was released as the play opened?[3] The answers to these questions help to delineate the aesthetics of his adaptation. As Lieber recounts, it was the screenwriter and translator Paule de Beaumont who—along with the producers Pierre Lazareff and Hervé Mille—secured the rights to the play and asked Cocteau to get involved in the French production. Beaumont would later translate *The Rose Tattoo* and *Summer and Smoke*[4] by herself, but in the case of *Streetcar*, after having discovered the play on Broadway, she felt that Cocteau's fame and his recognized talents as a poet were necessary to introduce Williams to Paris: "Tennessee Williams was unknown in France, the play daring for the times; we needed a prestigious name. We were all very close with Jean Cocteau and we thought he was the one who, working from my translation, could write an adaptation worthy

of the play," she recalls ("Tennessee Williams était inconnu en France, la
pièce osée pour l'époque, il fallait un nom prestigieux. Nous étions les uns
et les autres très liés avec Jean Cocteau et nous avons pensé qu'il était celui
qui, à partir de ma traduction, pouvait en faire une adaptation digne de
la pièce").[5] Cocteau had neither read nor seen the play when he accepted,
but he did attend a performance of Kazan's production in New York
before starting work on the French text.[6] His dedication to the project was
also heightened by personal ties, since Rouleau had previously directed
Cocteau's *The Typewriter* in 1941, while Cocteau's lover and muse, Jean
Marais, was initially considered for the part of Stanley (Bak 128). Beyond
penning the text, Cocteau attended rehearsals, gave interviews, wrote a
note in the program, and drew several lithographs for the Bordas edition,
evoking the silhouettes of Rouleau's production in his unmistakable technique of stylized classicism.

By his own admission, Cocteau's command of English was not precise
enough to allow for poetic nuance: "My English is too poor to express
the complex shades of meaning required by my work" ("Mon anglais est
trop pauvre pour exprimer les nuances difficiles auxquelles mon métier
m'oblige"; Cocteau, *Lettre* 42). Though he did work with the original
Streetcar playtext as well as Beaumont's version, his *Tramway* was thus
conceived as an "adaptation" based on Beaumont's "translation" ("adaptation de Jean Cocteau d'après la traduction de Paule de Beaumont"). The
indirect method proved highly problematic in terms of precision of meaning, though it led to happier results in terms of poetic quality. The play,
as Paris heard it for the first time, was marred by glaring mistakes due to
excessive literalness, sometimes to the point of transliterating sound at the
expense of meaning. For instance, Blanche's request that Stella should not
look at her "till later, not till I've bathed and rested" (251) was inaccurately
rendered as "un peu plus tard, après un bain et le reste" ("after my bath and
everything else"; 21): the translator's "reste" (mis)interprets the English
word *rest* in its sense of "and the rest" and thus sounds like the original
"rested" but means something entirely different. In contrast, the sound
of the English was sometimes ignored exactly when it seems important:
Stanley's voluptuously soothing words to Stella "Now, now, love" (419)
were surprisingly translated according to the temporal meaning of "now":

"*maintenant, maintenant* mon amour" (215), the italics perhaps indicating awareness of the mistranslation or possibly even a deliberate choice. Such sporadic errors in the text range from shifting the meaning of a line ("what's he like?" [258] becomes "what *does* he like?" when translated as "Qu'est-ce qui lui plaît?" [31]) to altering the weight of a scene, as when the passing youth whom Blanche flirts with in scene 5 appears more grown-up in French through his mistranslated taste in drinks.[7] Instead of taking shelter in a "drugstore," the young man walks into a "bistro," where instead of a "cherry soda" (338) he orders a "sherry" (128), which makes Blanche's flirting sound less transgressive, all the while domesticating the cultural references and canceling part of their Americanness. In "Les passagers du *Tramway nommé Désir* sont habités par le rêve" ("The Passengers of *Streetcar Named Desire* Are Haunted by Dreams"), an article Cocteau published in a Paris newspaper a few days before the production premiered, the author poetically stated that he had translated *Streetcar* "the way blind people read, walking [his] fingers over the slightest embossed design of the text" ("comme lisent les aveugles, en promenant mes doigts sur les moindres reliefs du texte"), and it would be easy, with such examples, to catch him in the trap of his own simile, since at times his dialogue plainly lacks clear-sightedness. While it is difficult to say exactly where to lay the blame for these misconceptions—on Beaumont, Cocteau, or their joint decisions—they explain why this particular text was not taken up by later editions. Beaumont preferred to be the sole translator of Librairie Théâtrale's 1977 version of *Tramway*, regularly reprinted since then.

Cocteau as Privileged Interpreter

Despite these flaws in the adaptation process, asking Cocteau to translate Williams was more than a marketing ploy to lure in the Parisian audience, reassuring them as to the literary quality of a foreign play—it was a relevant aesthetic intuition. A seasoned dramatist in his own right, Cocteau made sure the text Rouleau's actors performed was stageworthy in its rhythms and its evocations, paying great attention to word order and to building dialogic tension.[8] Furthermore, his own aesthetics coincided with those of Williams in revealing ways. Both Cocteau and Williams were "hybrid" artists, interested in several forms of writing and in the visual arts as well (Michiels and Collard 505). Their contributions to the seventh art (i.e., cinema) and their status as public figures led them both to preside over the Cannes Film Festival. More important, they shared what Jean Kontaxopoulos calls an "intellectual affinity" of the kind that fosters artistic correspondences: Kontaxopoulos identifies them as twentieth-century "poètes maudits" ("cursed poets") and notes their shared preoccupation with the figure of Orpheus as a vector for autobiographical sublimation (of homosexuality in particular), while Laura Michiels and Christophe Collard highlight a "reciprocal relation of artistic attraction and resistance" between their works (506). More specifically, Cocteau's *The Eagle Has Two Heads* has been cited as an influence on Williams's *The Milk Train Doesn't Stop Here Any More* (Debusscher, "French Stowaways") as well as on some of the language in *Streetcar* (Bak). John Bak also convincingly points to Cocteau's and Williams's symmetrical sensitivity to "the tragedy of incomprehension"—that original human tragedy that can be said to drive the plots of both *Streetcar* and *Eagle* (280–81). Sophie Maruéjouls-Koch posits another similarity in dramatic motivation when she argues that *Streetcar* and Cocteau's film *Beauty and the Beast* can be read as "two subversive rewritings of the same tale" of sublimated desires ("*La Belle et la Bête* et *A Streetcar Named Desire* apparaissent [. . .] comme les réécritures subversives d'un même conte"; 8). Cocteau and Williams rarely met, never got on especially well, and never collaborated[9]—but they admired each other's work, and the points of coincidence between their arts may have led Cocteau to feel rather confident in interpreting the play he was translating by the light of his own aesthetics.

Adding to the aforementioned literary kinships, I would argue that Cocteau saw in the contrast between Blanche and Stanley a variation on his lifelong obsession with the ambiguous figure of the angel, which he kept drawing, writing, and staging throughout his career. From the herald angel of his early poetic works to the angelic characters threatened by dwarves or beasts in his more famous films, the figure exists in constant tension, hovering between rising and falling to earth, an ambivalent dynamic between the angel as object of desire and the fearsome angel of death. It is not mere chance that the word "ange" is used again and again as a term of endearment in Cocteau's *Tramway*, from the first scene to the last. Marielle Wyns analyzes Cocteau's angel as a protean and androgynous creature, which calls to mind Williams's and Cocteau's tendency to identify with their female protagonists (Kontaxopoulos), and which in some ways prefigures Tony Kushner's use of the angel motif. We could also note, as far as androgyny is concerned, that Cocteau poetically does not correct the grammatical mistake in "Belle Reve" (which allies a feminine adjective with a masculine noun), preferring to let the name resonate as both French and foreign, male and female, echoing at the same time the name of his own most famous heroine, Belle of *La Belle et la Bête*. "[B]orn of the imagination of a smoker," Cocteau's angel "frequently oscillates between elevation and depths" ("l'ange coctalien, né de l'imaginaire d'un fumeur, [. . .] oscille souvent entre élévation et profondeur"; Wyns 225), a tension between two poles that is clearly reflected in Cocteau's perception of *Streetcar*'s main characters:

> All of [Williams's] characters are haunted by dreams, and they express it through tenderness, lying, anger, or silence.
>
> The poetry of *Streetcar* resembles the steam which rises from the Kowalskis' bathroom, where Blanche hums and simmers. It places a kind of tulle veil between audience and stage, analogous to those actual tulles which create a set out of thin air, enabling us to inhabit both the rooms and the street. [. . .]
>
> Because *Streetcar* is immersed in poetry, the unpleasant characters become the most pleasant ones. The same thing happens when the Duke and Duchess crush Don Quixote and Sancho under the weight of all their cleverness and luxurious pranks. Don Quixote and Sancho emerge as angels.
>
> Angels—that is the proper word for Blanche Dubois, the crazy woman, and Stanley, the gorilla. The core of their soul is made of crystal. It is through them that the other characters of the drama move and act.

> Tous ses personnages sont habités par du rêve et l'expriment avec la tendresse, le mensonge, la colère, le silence.
>
> La poésie de "Streetcar" ressemble à cette buée qui s'échappe de la salle de bains des Kowalsky, où Blanche chantonne et mijote. Elle met entre le spectateur et le spectacle une sorte de tulle analogue à ceux qui plantent le décor dans le vide et permettent de vivre dans les chambres et dans la rue.

> Grâce à la poésie qui baigne "Streetcar," les personnages antipathiques deviennent les plus sympathiques. C'est ce qui se passe lorsque le duc et la duchesse écrasent Don Quichotte et Sancho de leur intelligence et de leurs farces luxueuses. Don Quichotte et Sancho en sortent comme des anges.
>
> Anges sont Blanche Dubois, la folle, et Stanley, le gorille. Le bloc de leur âme est de cristal. C'est à travers eux que les autres personnages du drame se meuvent et agissent. (Cocteau, "Les passagers")

Such a poetic depiction of the plot opposes Blanche and Stanley in their personalities but reunites them in an essentialized mode of incarnation. Rouleau echoes this idea when he states in an interview that the struggle between Stanley and Blanche symbolically represents "the struggle between flesh and spirit" ("C'est la lutte entre la chair et l'esprit"; Fo), pointing to a French interpretation of the play built around heightened oppositions.

Sharpening the Contrasts

The heightened opposition is palpable in the translated text. The idea of the characters' souls as "made of crystal" encourages Cocteau to choose the lyric over the prosaic in key moments, as is shown in the treatment of two of the play's revelations. The first, from scene 7, delivered by Stella:

> This beautiful and talented young man was a degenerate. (*Streetcar* 364)

> Son demi-dieu aimait les garçons. [Her demigod preferred boys.] (*Tramway* 156)

And the second, from scene 9, delivered by Blanche:

> After the death of Allan—intimacies with strangers was all I seemed able to fill my empty heart with. . . . (*Streetcar* 386)

> Après la mort d'Alain, il m'a semblé que seuls les inconnus pouvaient m'aveugler le cœur! [After the death of Allan, it seemed to me that only strangers could make my heart blind!] (*Tramway* 181)

Cocteau poetizes the revelation of Allan's homosexuality; his choice of words is as explicit as it is free of judgment. While the label "degenerate" implies rejection and the disgust with her own disgust that drives Blanche to madness, Cocteau's clearer words are idealized, condensed in a short, expressive sentence that resonates almost like a saying, irrevocable. The violence of the English is equaled in French by the finality of the line, but not by any sort of condemnation. In the second revelation, Blanche's admission of promiscuity is euphemized by the disappearance of the word "intimacies," while the ordinary idea of "fill[ing]" one's heart is replaced by the more literary metaphor of sight and by the idea—one dear to Cocteau—of voluntarily "blind[ing]" one's heart. Grammatically speaking, the agency shifts from the first person ("I") to the third ("les inconnus," meaning "strange" or "unknown" men), making the line sound more like the confession of a distraught victim than a predator. This lyrical tendency is magnified by the rhythm of the French line, which is one syllable short of scanning like two alexandrines—that most recognizable of meters to French ears, which Cocteau had used in his verse play *Renaud et Armide*. The balance of the first part of the line is upset by the missing syllable in the second half, echoing in words the dissonance of Blanche's life. Once again, the point is not to hide the shocking facts of the plot, which elsewhere are exaggerated—immediately afterward, in the recording, Blanche mentions the fifteen-year-old boy she had an affair with (rather than seventeen, as in the English and the French published texts). The intent is, rather, to enhance Blanche's suffering by intensifying the contrasts. Such literary choices in the adaptation are perceptible throughout the text, especially in key lines and monologues, where the mode of expression is more intimate.

In an effort to compensate for this poetic treatment of soliloquies and approach the easy informality of Williams's text, Cocteau juxtaposes a number of slang words in the dialogue. For instance, when Stanley says "I want my baby," Cocteau writes "je veux ma gosse" (90), which literally means "I want my brat." In Parisian argot, "gosse" ("brat") was used as a term of endearment for one's girlfriend—and can indeed be heard in a number of old-fashioned popular songs—so Cocteau's choice, in addition to being idiomatic, immediately places the scene on the streets of Montmartre. What critics have mostly found fault with, though, is not the slang but the vulgarity of Cocteau's translation, especially after Williams complained in an interview that he didn't understand why Cocteau had stuffed his play with so many swear words (Delpech). It is a fact that the French version unnecessarily amplifies the coarseness of the text at times, as when Stanley says, "I never met a woman that didn't know if she was good-looking or not without being told" (278), and Cocteau offers "J'ai jamais rencontré une poule qui ne savait pas à quoi s'en tenir sur sa gueule" (56), where "une poule" is closer to "a broad," and "sa gueule" is an uncouth word for "face," making Stanley sound needlessly insulting ("I never met a broad who didn't know exactly what to think of her damn face").

However, the recording also shows that the occasional use of the word "merde" ("shit"), which has been ironically read as a French caricature of American orality, does not coarsen the register as much as one might think, since the actors often deliver it humorously. Eunice shouts it in self-derision as she slams the door, causing the audience to laugh, and the replacement of Stanley's exasperated "Now let's cut the re-bop!" (280) in scene 2 by "Merde!" (57) is, surprisingly, quite effective in performance. In the recording, Arletty's Blanche has been droning on flirtatiously, with meticulous diction, when Yves Vincent's Stanley cuts her off with his gruff exclamation, delivered simply, and stops her mannered conversation in midstream. At this point, Cocteau's published text follows Williams's original, in which Blanche, *pressing her hands to her ears,* exclaims "Ouuuuu!" (though Cocteau explicitly describes this frightened reaction as "feigned" —in his version, Blanche covers her ears "avec une intimidation feinte"). In the recorded performance, however, Vincent exclaims "Merde!," and Arletty, instead of cringing, immediately comes back with "Perfect!" ("Parfait!"), suggesting that Stanley's vulgar expletive tells her everything she needs to know about his personality. Her aloof commentary on Stanley's boorish attitude gets another laugh and encourages the audience to side with her as she proceeds to say that she has nothing to hide. In this instance, Cocteau and Rouleau can be charged with tipping the scales in Blanche's favor, but not with betraying the register, which is idiomatic and contrasted rather than truly indecorous.

The discrepancy between Williams's tonality and Cocteau's version lies perhaps not so much in specific choices or drops in the register but rather in the organicity of the play's language. Williams's dialogue is at once everyday and poetic, whereas Cocteau juxtaposes the everyday and the poetic, compensating a lyrical period with a coarser expression in the next line. The effect is slightly decentering and illustrates the two extremes of the fourth "deforming tendenc[y]" of translation that Antoine Berman outlines in "Translation and the Trials of the Foreign" (288): the tendency to either ennoble or popularize. As Berman notes, most translators of literary prose succumb to either or both of these temptations. That Cocteau, in succumbing to both, does so with a poet's command of words and rhythm only throws into sharper relief the contrasts in register, cadence, and mood that his version intensifies throughout the play.

Exoticizing *la Nouvelle Orléans*

A crucial problem facing any French production of Tennessee Williams—to this day—is atmosphere, as rendered through sets, accents, attitudes, and music. Convincingly re-creating in Paris the "*raffish charm*" of the play's set, where "[*y*]*ou can almost feel the warm breath of the brown river*" and hear the "*tinny piano being played with the infatuated fluency of brown fingers*" (243), is no small challenge, especially on the relatively small stage of the Théâtre Édouard VII in 1949, in front of an audience that, as Lewis Falb has shown, tended to assimilate anything that came from the United States with the Old West. (For instance, although the plot of Eugene O'Neill's *Desire under the Elms* is set in New England, French critics repeatedly assumed that it took place west of the Mississippi, in regions associated in the popular imagination with ranches and cowboy hats [10].) While Williams's opening stage direction, with its celebrated use of lyricism and synesthesia, is drastically shortened in Cocteau's published version, the accounts of the production unanimously agree that the set was remarkably authentic and suggestive. "You can not only see New Orleans, you can just about smell it," Dorsey writes in his review, going so far as to conjecture that the old spring rocker and the broken-down cane chairs must have been imported for the occasion. The set had been created by the Italian designer and fashion illustrator Lila de Nobili, who was later to design other Rouleau productions of US plays, such as *Orpheus Descending* and *The Crucible*. Her design for *Streetcar*—a sketch of which appeared in the French *Vogue*—was constructed to enable fluid transitions between scenes, thus doing justice to Williams's cinematographic composition. The front of the stage represented the two rooms of the Kowalskis' apartment, with a staircase to the side leading up to Steve and Eunice's place and to a gallery that ran across the stage. The description of the radio commentator, Charles Oulmont, makes clear the ways Rouleau used this gallery to stage mimed transitions between the main scenes enacted downstairs. These interludes showed Eunice cooking on the gallery with a dancing step, feeding and kissing her children, or being pursued by Steve, always to jazz music, and always as a counterpoint to the main action below, suggesting a constant swarming, intrusive activity around the Kowalskis' apartment. The actress chosen to play Eunice, Milly Mathis, was undoubtedly cast because of her cheerfully comical southern personality and thick Marseillais accent, which immediately made her recognizable as the loud, friendly, and emotional type she had played in Marcel Pagnol's movies. Rouleau was not trying to transplant the play to the French South—Milly Mathis was the only one with a southern accent, and the lead actors' voices were typically Parisian—but he was relying on his Provençal Eunice, hovering in the gallery above, to foster a certain sense of familiarity, just as he was relying on the infectious laughter of the young comedian Louis de Funès, as Pablo, to liven the mood at the opening of the poker game.

De Nobili's set had another remarkable feature: the back wall of the Kowalskis' apartment was a scrim that the lighting could render transparent. In between scenes, the wall melted away to reveal the street behind—peopled by sailors, children, street vendors, and black dancers—the set thus materializing the porosity of the border between public and private spheres that cruelly unpeels Blanche's secrets. The street also became noisy with shouts, snatches of songs, and the sound of the streetcar whenever it took visual shape, creating beautiful and evocative tableaux. However lively and picturesque this representation of New Orleans was, though, its impact could not be the same in Paris as in New York, and what Williams wrote as natural and recognizable was translated by Cocteau and Rouleau as thrillingly exotic. Compare the introduction of the first two characters in the English and French versions:

Two women, one white and one colored, are taking the air on the steps of the building. The white woman is Eunice, who occupies the upstairs flat; the colored woman a neighbor, for New Orleans is a cosmopolitan city where there is a relatively warm and easy intermingling of races in the old part of town. (*Streetcar* 243)

Une grande négresse languide est assise sur l'escalier, s'éventant avec une feuille de palmier ainsi qu'Eunice Hubben, locataire de l'appartement du dessus. [*A tall languid Negro woman is sitting on the stairs, fanning herself with a palm leaf, along with Eunice Hubben, who lives upstairs.*] (*Tramway* 12)

Cocteau does not bother to translate Williams's realistic precisions about the population of New Orleans, preferring to evoke a more romanticized vision of far-off lands. The adjective "languid" and the addition of the palm leaf—which Cocteau also drew in the corner of his lithographs for the play—seem to conjure up the mysteriously tropical landscapes of Baudelaire's "La vie antérieure." The intertext here is artistic rather than foreign. Interestingly, exoticizing the context of the play is a recurring directorial gesture in French productions of *Streetcar*. When Lee Breuer directed the play at the Comédie Française in 2011, he chose to approach Blanche's nostalgia for the Old South, with its codes and its aristocratic elegance, through the metaphor of Japanese orientalism, presenting a "Kabuki-like Blanche," so as to "mak[e] it clear that the play is not a naturalistic tragedy but a metatheatrical dream play about the staging of fantasy" (Savran 275). The choice was daring and unexpected but extremely effective in performance. Well aware that any linguistic or cultural connection between France and New Orleans is far too tenuous to be a shared reference, French productions of *Streetcar* seem to prefer to increase the distance, using it as poetic symbolism, rather than reduce it.

The attitude of Cocteau's "grande négresse languide"[10] also points to one of the more polemic aspects of Rouleau's staging: the association of black bodies and desire. According to the radio commentary, a black female belly dancer first appeared behind the scrim after Stanley takes Stella to their bedroom at the end of scene 3, in a heavily symbolic interlude set to rapid drumbeats, before Blanche ventures downstairs in search of her sister. A similar episode recurred, with more dancers, at the end of scene 4 after Stella kisses Stanley, and at the end of scene 9 during the night of the rape. A questionable conceit, this embodiment of eroticism was derided by many a critic, not least amusingly by Truman Capote, who called the staging "chichi beyond words," elucidating that "on all those occasions when Stanley is supposed to be getting those colored lights going the stage is flooded with Negros doing belly-shakes—ludicrous" (102). Capote reads the "frantic Negro dances" ("danses nègres folles"), to quote Oulmont's description, as metaphors of Stanley's brutal desire. But it is in fact unclear whether they were meant to be associated strictly with Stanley—materializing as they did at every expression of his sexuality—or also with Blanche's ambivalent attraction-repulsion to his masculinity, the undulating black dancers offering a liberating foil to her "white" dress and name (which in French persistently rings as a color). Philip C. Kolin has interestingly suggested that Rouleau's production "anticipated by almost fifty years" recent racial readings of *Streetcar* that attribute the characteristics of black people to Stanley, the "Polack" (72). A passage from *A Letter to Americans*, which Cocteau wrote on the plane back from his New York trip in early 1949, sheds further light on this point:

> Americans,
>
> You brush against the real world. Your sects, your clandestine religions, your ghosts, your fevers, your anguish, your worrying, your crimes, and even your dread of Harlem and its beautiful dances, all speak volumes to me about your desire. And you are ashamed of it. And you hide it. And you go out to get a whiff of it from dark shows which secretly feed you.
>
> I saw you, Americans, leaving your seats at the end of Tennessee Williams's *A Streetcar Named Desire*, shamefaced and gratified, observing each other out of the corner of your eye, seeing your wives and daughters swooning in the arms of that extraordinary actor, Marlon Brando.

> Américains,
>
> Vous frôlez le vrai monde. Vos sectes, vos religions clandestines, vos fantômes, vos fièvres, votre angoisse, votre inquiétude, vos crimes, et jusqu'à votre effroi de Harlem aux belles danses, me renseignent sur votre désir. Et vous en avez honte. Et vous le dissimulez. Et vous allez le renifler dans des spectacles troubles qui vous nourrissent en cachette.

Je vous ai vus, Américains, quitter vos places à la fin de *A street Car named Desire* de Tennessee Williams, honteux et comblés, vous observant du coin de l'œil, voyant vos femmes et vos filles à la renverse entre les bras de l'extraordinaire acteur Marlon Brando. (55)

Both the dancing bodies of Harlem and the talents of Marlon Brando are alluded to as objects of admiration and apprehension. The black dancer, whom Cocteau associates with beauty, becomes a metaphor not just for the characters' desire but for America's secret longings and fears. Rouleau's production literalized this vision, revealing and celebrating, behind the scrim of propriety, what Cocteau read (or fantasized) as the forbidden desire of a nation.

Arletty's Enigmatic Blanche

Let us turn to what was undeniably the production's greatest success in French eyes: Arletty's incarnation of Blanche. Casting a fifty-year-old actor as Blanche was a bold choice, though by no means an exceptional one— Krzysztof Warlikowski recently cast another French star, Isabelle Huppert, in the same role at fifty-seven (Lemoine)—but thanks to Arletty's talent and persona,[11] her Blanche turned out to be a sensation. Her sense of comedy, working-class Paris accent, and fine legs had garnered Arletty praise and popularity in various operettas in the 1930s, though she had graduated to darker roles and a mysterious aura on screen during the war. Marcel Carné cast her as the self-sacrificing Clara in the tragic love tangles of *Le jour se lève* and as the dangerously seductive Dominique, the devil's envoy, in *Les visiteurs du soir*, a role she defined as a "turning point in [her] career," changing her typical part "from the lighter character to the more enigmatic one" ("Ce fut un tournant dans ma carrière [. . .]: je passais du personnage léger au personnage énigmatique"; 134). Both films had been penned by Jacques Prévert, associating Arletty's status as a star with her chiseled rendering of his studied words and poetic images (shedding her accent when needed). This association was confirmed by her consecration in Carné and Prévert's wartime masterpiece, *Les enfants du paradis*, where she portrayed the charismatic Garance, in a role that began with her sitting naked in a tub and ended with a shot of her queenlike face, hieratic and beautiful, turning away from the man she loved, thereby forgoing her own happiness. Arletty was (and consciously staged herself as) both a woman of the flesh and a woman of magnificent attitudes, fluent in literary lines and in argot, which made her well suited to portray Blanche's ambivalence. Wearing "a mask of dignity (that of lies)" and yet "betraying here and there flashes of sensuality, of degradation" ("l'actrice [. . .] doit à la fois porter un masque de dignité (celui du mensonge) et pourtant laisser passer çà et là des éclairs de sensualité, d'avilissement"; Maurois), Arletty performed what composed overall a "highly distinguished" and "delicate" interpreta-tion ("figure très racée"; "style [. . .] délicat"; Kemp). As the role lost its southern roots in her Parisian incarnation, it became more universal in its resonance: "Arletty's Blanche, necessarily, is any down-at-heels aristocrat decaying in poverty anywhere—in these times she could be Russian, Polish or even Chinese," Dorsey writes, and this universality goes hand in hand with Cocteau's adaptation of Blanche's reverie on her own name in scene 3:

> It's a French name. It means woods and Blanche means white, so the two together mean white woods. Like an orchard in spring! (*Streetcar* 299)

> C'est un nom français. (*Puis, comme dans un rêve*) Cela veut dire: Forêt blanche. La dame de la forêt. La dame blanche. [It's a French name. (*Then, as in a dream*) It means: White forest. The lady of the forest. The lady in white.] (*Tramway* 81)

A literal translation of the line would be superfluous in French, but Cocteau's way out of this difficulty is significant: he chooses to highlight the mythical, trading Blanche's Mississippi origins for a legendary aura of femininity, associating whiteness with the darkness of night by adding a stage direction that invokes "*un rêve*." Arletty delivers the line with-out coquettishness, in an almost monotonous voice that does justice to Cocteau's indication of a dreamlike quality, contributing to what the press celebrated as the actor's "power of fascination" ("un pouvoir fascinateur"; Maulnier).

Arletty's personal history is also a factor in her impact on French audiences in 1949. Not unlike Blanche, Arletty had lost her first love tragically—in World War I, after which she vowed never to marry—and subsequently had a series of more or less scandalous liaisons, the most infamous being her passionate affair with Hans Jürgen Soehring, a high-ranking officer in the Luftwaffe, during the German occupation. She had been on trial after the liberation, occasioning a famously brazen retort (in reality suggested to her by the scriptwriter Henri Jeanson): "My heart is French, my ass is international" ("Mon cœur est français, mon cul est international"; Arletty 29). The Comité d'épuration had banned her from working for three years, which means that *Streetcar* was her grand return into the public eye after much controversy. A dramatic part that unites dark secrets with sincere longings for love was an apt choice; Arletty's fear of failure mirrored Blanche's, and the French critics' approval of her performance was also a way to welcome her back, lauding her acting talents above Williams's writing. Arletty's love life even had an impact on the text since, in the light of her situation, she staunchly refused to say "I have always depended on the kindness of strangers" the way Cocteau had initially rendered it. Cocteau's original translation, "J'ai toujours suivi les étrangers" ("I have always followed strangers"; qtd. in Arletty 130), had used the most natural French translation for "strangers"—"étrangers." The word *étranger*, however, also means "foreigner" and could have gotten Arletty booed on her exit. On her insistence, the text was altered to "J'ai toujours suivi des inconnus" ("unknown men" or "persons"; *Tramway* 214; Arletty 130). The line loses some of its power in the French version, since the poetic idea of depending on someone's kindness is replaced by the simpler, factual image of following someone. Arletty, however, rendered it compelling and regal nonetheless, her delivery convincingly ladylike, with only a hint of seductiveness.

Arletty's exit was regal indeed: Cocteau adds to scene 11 a stage direction that explicitly announces itself as a deviation from Williams's script, specifically for the French production: "In France, Blanche finishes the play wearing her ball gown, with a tiara on her head" ("En France Blanche termine la pièce en robe de bal, son diadème sur la tête"; 203). This addition is illustrated by the lithograph on an unnumbered page between pages 208 and 209, where Cocteau's minimalist lines sketch out a triumphant silhouette sweeping out on the doctor's arm, head held high, the train of her dress ruffling behind her, liberated and vindicated in her fantasies finally come true.

The French production openly intended to readjust the play's balance in Blanche's favor, highlighting "the intense inner life which makes her a person gifted with greatness and poetry" ("sa vie intérieure intense qui en fait une personne douée de grandeur et de poésie"; 111). Cocteau advertised this intention in an interview: "The play was written with a marvelous role for a woman. [B]ut Marlon Brando—I think perhaps he is the best actor in the United States—was so good that he overshadowed her. But here the woman's role [. . .] will be more important than in the United States" (qtd. in "Shipping News"). Getting the audience to side with Blanche was all the easier since Vincent, though a competent actor with a successful movie career ahead of him, was "badly miscast," as Dorsey's review describes him. (Most reviews simply omitted any discussion of Vincent's performance, which in itself is telling.) Indeed, in the recording Vincent's Stanley sounds much more well-behaved and articulate than Brando (who had come to a week of rehearsals and unsuccessfully tried to perform the role in phonetic French). I would tentatively suggest that the hardest part to cast in transla-tion is not Blanche—despite the missing cliché of the southern belle—but Stanley. Actors from different countries may successfully embody very different Blanches, since the image of the fallen lady, or the woman with secrets, speaks easily across time and cultures; Stanley's blend of ease and brutality—and its relation to his specific class status in the United States in the mid-twentieth century—is much harder to adapt without weakening or caricaturing him.

Arletty's Blanche, undoubtedly, was less physically and vocally fragile than Jessica Tandy's or Vivien Leigh's. Unlike most actors who embodied the part early in the play's history, she did not bleach her hair to appear more mothlike and did not emulate southern inflections, keeping instead a low register of voice, occasionally discordant, alternating seductive musical intonations with long toneless speeches that spoke both to her exhaustion and to her descent into fantasy. This "voix blanche" ("toneless voice," liter-ally "white voice"), as a critic described it, proved at once compelling and moving: "Almost without a gesture, almost without an intonation, using a style of performing one might call neutral, a toneless voice that sometimes becomes grating, a peal of broken laughter, she reaches an expressive intensity that means the audience cannot take their eyes off her for a second" ("Presque sans geste, presque sans intonations, avec un jeu pour ainsi dire neutre, une voix blanche et un peu grinçante, un petit rire fêlé, elle atteint à une intensité d'expression qui fait que le spectateur ne peut pas la lâcher une seconde"; Maulnier). The end of scene 5 is particularly convincing in the recording, as Arletty uses a bewitching voice, silky-soft in its low tones, to seduce the young man, letting her desperation ring out only in the louder and less refined "Hé!" she repeatedly uses to detain him as he offers to leave. After the young man's exit, her voice rises a full octave to welcome Mitch, betraying the artifice of their courtship. Other deeply compelling passages are her drained monologue about death at Belle Reve (scene 1) and her masterful speech comparing Stanley to an ape (scene 4), both of which were adapted by Cocteau with an ear for rhythm and gradation, to which she does perfect justice, rising and falling in intensity with the periods, wavering between authority and entreaty. There is something forceful in Arletty's Blanche and her superior use of intonation, as is confirmed by a telling alteration made to the script in scene 6 of the recording. Instead of comparing herself to Marguerite in *La dame aux camélias* (as Blanche does in both Williams's original ["*Je suis la Dame aux Camellias! Vous êtes—Armand!* Understand French?*"; 344] and Cocteau's published text ["Je suis la Dame aux Camélias, vous êtes Armand Duval"; 134]), Arletty's Blanche picks a much stronger heroine to identify with, casting herself as Carmen and Mitch as Don José. (Whether Arletty herself made the change or, more likely, Rouleau made it [or asked Cocteau to come up with something different during rehearsals] is impossible to know.) The dialogue that can be heard in the recording is as follows:

> BLANCHE: Vive la bohème! Ah! Nous sommes à Séville, à
> la terrasse d'un café. Je suis Carmen, vous êtes Don José.
>
> MITCH: Moi?
>
> BLANCHE: *¿Quieres dormir esta noche? ¿Conmigo? ¿Comprendes? ¿No?* C'est une vraie chance!

When the French is translated directly into English, the passage reads:

> BLANCHE: Long live Bohemia! Ah! We're sitting at the terrace of a café in Seville. I am Carmen. You are Don José.

MITCH: Me?

BLANCHE: *¿Quieres dormir esta noche? ¿Conmigo?*
¿Comprendes? ¿No? That's a good thing!

Arletty's Blanche does not have the intense vulnerability of Marguerite Gautier, but her fall is all the more moving, making the actor a distinguished ambassador of the character's complexities to postwar French audiences.

Almost seven decades after Cocteau and Rouleau's *Tramway*, their choices still prove intriguing, which is a testament to their daring take on Williams's text. I would argue that, rather than an odd premiere to be regarded as somewhat misguided in the French journey of the play, the production was instead the pioneering first of several highly personal approaches to *Streetcar* staged by French theaters, in which many of Cocteau and Rouleau's directorial gestures recurred: exoticizing the context, for example; or using a famous actor's star power to concentrate a wealth of fantasies around the figure of Blanche (Warlikowski's and Breuer's twenty-first-century productions do both). Perhaps because of *Streetcar*'s distinctly American flavor and immediately iconic status, French productions do not simply undertake to "serve" the text but strive instead to reinvent it. While *Streetcar*'s Hollywood adaptation may have generated the play's true popularity in France, Cocteau and Rouleau had, from the start, more finely defined the elements that made for its eventual success with French audiences. They had also anticipated the play's pitfalls for French adaptations, however surprising their responses might seem. Cocteau's concept of *Streetcar* may be too much his own dream about the play to be used for another production, just as his script is too fraught with translation errors to be reprinted without corrections, but his adaptation remains a carefully crafted and poetic text, staged in full awareness of its scandalous and controversial potential. In fact, this potential for controversy probably contributed to the choice to stage it. Reviews should not be taken as the definitive image of the production, then or now, since, as Cocteau well knew, "France is now one of the only countries where the crowd can make a success of a play on the grounds that the critics condemn it" ("La France actuellement est un des seuls pays où la foule puisse faire le succès d'une pièce parce que les journalistes la condamnent"; Cocteau, *Lettre* 83).

Notes

I am indebted to Marc Robinson for asking me if I was familiar with Cocteau's text, thus prompting me to dig in the archives of the Bibliothèque nationale de France (BNF) and giving me the idea for this paper.

[1] The play premiered at the Théâtre Édouard VII on 17 Oct. 1949.

[2] "Ertderg" is MacColl's mocking representation of the word "hot dog" as pronounced by French actors.

[3] Nowadays Bordas specializes in classic textbooks and dictionaries, but in 1949 it was a young and innovative publishing house (founded in 1946). Not having been reprinted after 1949, Cocteau's text is rather hard to come by—even the BNF has it only on microfilm.

[4] Beaumont translated both *The Rose Tattoo* and *Summer and Smoke* in 1953. She also provided a literal translation of Eugene O'Neill's *Desire under the Elms* for the well-known French author Jean Anouilh to use in adapting the play in 1953.

[5] From a 1974 letter from Paule de Beaumont to Jean Dermit, qtd. in Lieber 154. Here and throughout, all translations and glosses from the French are my own unless otherwise specified.

[6] Cocteau's US trip, which inspired his *Lettre aux américains*, took place in December 1948–January 1949. Lieber quotes an 18 June 1949 letter to Jean Marais in which Cocteau states that he is "starting on *Streetcar*" ("Je me lance dans *Streetcar*"; 163).

[7] Cocteau restructures the play into acts, changing the scene numbers; for clarity's sake, the scene numbers used in this paper are Williams's.

[8] Lieber uses documents from the Cocteau archives in Montpellier to show that Cocteau made many corrections to the first draft for the sake of concision and dramatic efficiency, shortening sentences, reorganizing ideas, and making the text more suited to delivery by an actor (158–61).

[9] Both authors mention meeting each other in their memoirs, but only in passing and without any particular enthusiasm. It seems the kinship was literary rather than personal. Williams professed himself more interested in meeting Sartre when he discovered the bohemian nights of Paris in 1948: "I met Cocteau and Bésé Bérard and Jean Marais, and quite a lot of artists, but I was most interested in meeting Jean-Paul Sartre, whose existential philosophy appealed to me strongly, as did his play *Huit* [sic] *Clos*" (*Memoirs* 149). By contrast, Cocteau alludes to a later meeting in Barcelona in 1953, and condescendingly writes of his fellow poet: "Tennessee was always a little on the rough side, always rather far removed from what wasn't sexual" ("Tennesse toujours un peu coriace, un peu loin de ce qui n'est pas d'ordre sexuel"; from *Le passé défini*, qtd. in Lieber 153). Lieber notes that the exchanges between Cocteau and Williams do not appear to have been actively pursued by either author.

[10] It is worth noting that in 1949, in the wake of the Négritude movement, the term "négresse" is not the pejorative it is in other contexts. The clichéd literary exoticizing of the black neighbor and the black body is certainly questionable, but

the term itself was not intentionally derogatory (unlike its use in English at the time).

[11] I am using the concept of "persona" as defined for instance by George Toles, who analyzes "the persistence of the star persona—what audiences assume they know about an actor from his or her previous defining roles" (76). Toles persuasively argues that the back-and-forth between what the audience assumes and what the actor can bring to a new part is a fertile interaction.

Works Cited

Arletty. *Les mots d'Arletty*. Edited by Claudine Brécourt-Villars, Editions V et O, 1991.

Bak, John S. *Tennessee Williams: A Literary Life*. Palgrave Macmillan, 2013.

Berman, Antoine. "Translation and the Trials of the Foreign." Translated by Lawrence Venuti. *The Translation Studies Reader*, edited by Venuti, Routledge, 2000, pp. 284–97.

Capote, Truman. *Too Brief a Treat: The Letters of Truman Capote*. Edited by Gerald Clarke, Random House, 2004.

Cocteau, Jean. *Lettre aux américains*. Grasset, 1949.

——. "Les passagers du *Tramway nommé Désir* sont habités par le rêve." *Paris-Presse-L'Intransigeant*, 12 Oct. 1949.

Debusscher, Gilbert. "French Stowaways on an American Milk Train: Williams, Cocteau and Peyrefitte." *Modern Drama*, vol. 25, no. 3, Fall 1982, pp. 399–408.

Delpech, Jeanine. "Tennessee Williams à Paris." *Nouvelles Littéraires*, 8 June 1950.

Dorsey, Frank. "'Streetcar Named Desire' on the Boulevards." *New York Herald Tribune* [?], 19 Oct. 1949. Bibliothèque nationale de France, département Arts du spectacle, 8-RSUPP-2767, pp. 13–14, gallica.bnf.fr/ark:/12148 /btv1b105272052/f19.image.

Falb, Lewis. *American Drama in Paris, 1945–1970: A Study of Its Critical Reception*. U of North Carolina P, 1973.

Fo, J. "Arletty va conduire 'Un tramway nommé Désir.'" *Le Monde*, 12 Oct. 1949.

Hobson, Harold. "Miss Vivien Leigh." *Twentieth-Century Interpretations of* A Streetcar Named Desire: *A Collection of Critical Essays*, edited by Jordan Yale Miller, Prentice Hall, 1971, pp. 47–49. Originally published in *The Sunday Times* [London], 13 Nov. 1949.

Kemp, Robert. "Un tramway nommé désir." *Le Monde*, 19 Oct. 1949.

Kolin, Philip C. *Williams:* A Streetcar Named Desire. Cambridge UP, 2000.

Kontaxopoulos, Jean. "Orpheus Introspecting: Tennessee Williams and Jean Cocteau." *The Tennessee Williams Annual Review*, 2001, www.tennesseewilliamsstudies.org/journal/work.php?ID=36.

Lemoine, Xavier. "*Un Tramway*: Warlikowski's Desire to Reignite American Theatre in Europe." *Tennessee Williams and Europe: Intercultural Encounters, Transatlantic Exchanges*, edited by John S. Bak, Rodopi, 2014, pp. 323–43.

Lieber, Gérard. "La question de l'adaptation: L'exemple d'*Un tramway nommé Désir*." *Jean Cocteau, quarante ans après: 1963–2003*, edited by Pierre Caizergues, U Paul-Valéry, 2005, pp. 153–69.

MacColl, René. "Laughter dans le Tramway." *Twentieth-Century Interpretations of* A Streetcar Named Desire: *A Collection of Critical Essays*, edited by Jordan Yale Miller, Prentice Hall, 1971, pp. 49–52. Originally published in *The Atlantic Monthly*, July 1950, pp. 94–95.

Maruéjouls-Koch, Sophie. "Quand le théâtre s'inspire du cinéma: Jean Cocteau, Sergueï Eisenstein et Tennessee Williams." *Transatlantica*, vol. 1, 2015, journals.openedition.org/transatlantica/7529.

Maulnier, Thierry. "Une œuvre brutale, sensuelle, menée à la perfection." *La Bataille*, 20 Oct. 1949.

Maurois, André. "À propos d'"Un tramway nommé Désir."" *L'Aurore*, 20 Dec. 1949.

Michiels, Laura, and Christophe Collard. "Double Exposures: On the Reciprocity of Influence between Tennessee Williams and Jean Cocteau." *Comparative Drama*, vol. 47, no. 4, Winter 2013, pp. 505–27.

Savran, David. "The Kindness of Strangers?: Tennessee Williams in France and Germany." *Tennessee Williams and Europe: Intercultural Encounters, Transatlantic Exchanges*, edited by John S. Bak, Rodopi, 2014, pp. 259–78.

Shaw, Irwin. "Masterpiece." *Twentieth-Century Interpretations of* A Streetcar Named Desire: *A Collection of Critical Essays*, edited by Jordan Yale Miller, Prentice Hall, 1971, pp. 45–47. Originally published in *The New Republic*, 22 Dec. 1947, pp. 34–35.

"Shipping News." *New York Herald Tribune*, 14 Oct. 1949. Bibliothèque nationale de France, département Arts du spectacle, 8-RSUPP-2767, pp. 9–10, gallica.bnf.fr/ark:/12148/btv1b105272052/f15.image.

Toles, George. "'Brando Sings!': The Invincible Star Persona." *Theorizing Film Acting*, edited by Aaron Taylor, Routledge, 2012, pp. 76–89.

Verdot, Guy. "Un tramway nommé Désir et surnommé Patache." *Franc-Tireur*, 19 Oct. 1949.

Williams, Tennessee. *Memoirs*. Penguin, 2007.

——. *A Streetcar Named Desire*. 1947. *The Theatre of Tennessee Williams*, vol. 1, New Directions, 1971, pp. 239–419.

——. *Un tramway nommé Désir*. Adapted by Jean Cocteau from a translation by Paule de Beaumont, Bordas, 1949.

——. *Un tramway nommé Désir*. Radiodiffusion Française. *Archives Nationales de l'Audiovisuel*, www.ina.fr/audio/PHZ05046338. Recording of a performance at Théâtre Edouard VII, 16 Oct. 1949, with commentary by Charles Oulmont.

Wyns, Marielle. *Jean Cocteau: L'empreinte de l'ange*. L'Harmattan, 2005.

Tennessee Williams Wrestles with Race in Three Unpublished Works: "Goat Song," "Heavenly Grass," and "Why Did Desdemona Love the Moor?"

Tom Mitchell

Most of what is understood about Tennessee Williams's thoughts regarding his own white identity and the identities of racial others comes from his major published works, which often explore the topics more implicitly than explicitly. Issues of race and ethnicity form an important undercurrent running throughout his oeuvre, however, and the body of unpublished work produced in his career, which extended from the 1930s to the 1980s, includes enlightening deployment of non-white characters and overt exploration of racial themes. In some of these works—particularly during the early years, when Williams was attempting to establish himself as a playwright—his positions on racial justice, interracial romance, and the Ku Klux Klan were at odds with popular attitudes of his time. For a young writer attempting to get his career going in the period from 1936 to 1944, such themes may have been too risky, and may be part of the reason the works were neither published nor produced. Highlighting the straightforward racial perspective in three unpublished early works—the short plays "Goat Song" and "Heavenly Grass" and the short story "Why Did Desdemona Love the Moor?"—offers the critic insight into the evolution of the playwright's attitudes toward race and into the more subtle workings of race in the plays that made him famous.

Under consideration here are the short play "Goat Song," likely written in the late 1930s; "Heavenly Grass" (variously identified by Williams in the manuscript materials as "a primitive libretto," "a musical fantasy for the negro theatre," "a play with music," and "a negro folk opera"), probably written around 1941; and "Why Did Desdemona Love the Moor?," a short story that took shape between 1939 and 1943, at the same time he was writing *Battle of Angels*. Materials that make up these three works are found in the Tennessee Williams Collection of the Harry Ransom Center (HRC) at the University of Texas, Austin. All three contain plot and thematic elements that return in later work.

In adopting the identity of "Tennessee" at the beginning of his career, Thomas Lanier Williams chose to label himself a southern regional writer, and in so doing situated himself (consciously or not) in relation to various regional and national others. Critics such as Philip C. Kolin have long been interested in the significance of race to Williams's southern cultural identity and have documented many ways in which the playwright's references to race, fraught though they are with assumptions and prejudices, are "a reflection of his sympathetic views of the Other" (Kolin 204). Christopher Bigsby, for example, acknowledges that nonwhite characters appear infrequently in the major works, but uncovers a fundamental "contempt for the racist" through his detailed look at *Orpheus Descending* (36, 57–60). Nancy Tischler connects the oeuvre's kinship with marginalized characters (including racial minorities) to the playwright's feelings of isolation and oppression as a gay man and a poet from "the small-town, small-thinking South" (49). Fellow playwright Arthur Miller concurs: he writes that Williams saw himself as belonging to "a minority culture and understood in his bones what a brutal menace the majority could be if aroused against him" (180). The "fugitive kind" among whom Williams repeatedly casts himself includes African American, Mexican, Italian, German, and other groups who struggled (and often still struggle) against an oppressive society, suggesting that his depiction of racial others bears some relation to his own identity as a cultural outsider.

In an overview of the topic, Kolin identifies nonwhite characters appearing in the works most often referenced in discussions of Williams and race: dramatic works including *Battle of Angels*, *Orpheus Descending*, *Not about Nightingales*, *The Last of My Solid Gold Watches*, *Baby Doll*, *A Streetcar Named Desire*, and *Kingdom of Earth*; and the short fictions "Big Black: A Mississippi Idyll" and "Desire and the Black Masseur." *Streetcar* and its dangerous other, Stanley Kowalski, offer fertile ground for the critic: Mary F. Brewer (71–77), M. Tyler Sasser (154–60), and George Crandell (337–46) mine the play in depth for its implications about race, which, as in the larger body of Williams's work, are sometimes progressive, sometimes prone to the stereotypes and racist shorthand of the era. Crandell in particular provides an excellent analysis of Williams's use of African American characters, noting that the nonwhite characters are often marginal, subservient, or negatively depicted. Crandell finds that Williams's representation of African American characters participates in problematic approaches identified by Toni Morrison and George M. Fredrickson as common in works by (often well-meaning) white writers: Morrison observes that white writers often express a mixture of "fear and desire" regarding black characters, and Fredrickson coins the term "romantic racialists" to describe white writers who idealize nonwhite characters, endowing them with admirable qualities that the writers suggest the white community lacks (Crandell 342). Although focusing on *Streetcar*, Crandell goes on to identify these approaches throughout Williams's drama and fiction. The three unpublished works examined here show some of Williams's earliest attempts to represent blackness and its treatment by white society, and thus it seems helpful to list some of his formative experiences with racial issues and to provide their biographical and historical context.

Williams in Context: History and Race

Williams's childhood attitudes toward race would have developed under the simultaneous influence of the bigotry of his small delta town and the more enlightened view of his maternal grandfather, Reverend Walter Dakin, who, while not challenging the color line observed by the community, was reported to be uncharacteristically respectful of black citizens. The young Tom Williams spent his earliest years in the rectory of the Episcopal church served by Dakin, in Columbus, Mississippi. In his grandparents' home in Clarksdale, Mississippi, Williams grew up with an African American nurse, Ozzie, whose personality made a strong impression. His *Memoirs* records deep affection for her (11, 252), but his Mississippi upbringing also conditioned him to identify African Americans with subservient roles and to exert the power of his privilege. When he was four, Tom lashed out at Ozzie, calling her a "big, black nigger," an outburst he later regretted and that, according to his biographer Lyle Leverich, left him "with a lasting burden of guilt and shame" (43).

Although the family moved to St. Louis in 1918, the spiritual home remained in Clarksdale, deep in the Mississippi delta—a region notorious for racial violence and lynching in particular. The white-on-black violence prompted the Missouri Congressman Leonidas C. Dyer to introduce one of the first major pieces of anti-lynching legislation, a bill that would be passed by the US House of Representatives in 1918 but eventually halted in the Senate by southern senators (Thompson 90). During Williams's school-age years, from 1920 to 1929, there were sixty-four lynchings recorded in Mississippi and fifty more in the years 1930 to 1939. June 1934 saw a particularly horrific lynching just outside Clarksdale (Thompson 84, 98, 103). In fact, there were few places more associated with such violence than the delta region of Mississippi, though the *St. Louis Post-Dispatch* headlined a lynching in Maryville, Missouri, in January 1931 ("Negro Slayer" 1), while Williams was a student at the University of Missouri (an incident that would still be resounding nationwide in 1935, in an article in *Vanity Fair* [Gilmour]). Efforts to outlaw lynching continued to be thwarted, even though the Scottsboro Boys Trial in the 1930s raised awareness of bigotry and Klan intimidation. It is hard to imagine that Williams could have escaped the influence and effects of the racial bigotry behind the lynchings so close to home.

The St. Louis of Williams's school years was second only to Baltimore in the percentage of black citizens in its overall population (Heathcott 708). St. Louis dealt with the large number of African Americans moving up from the south by drawing housing boundaries and establishing seg-regation policies, divisions that plague the city to this day. The Williams family lived in the distinctly white Central West End of St. Louis, later moving into the nearby suburbs of University City and Clayton. The public schools of the time were segregated, and neither the University of Missouri nor Washington University was integrated until the early 1950s.

The University of Iowa (at the time called the State University of Iowa), which Williams attended in 1937–1938, was more progressive than its Missouri counterparts, its theater department particularly so. The Department of Speech and Dramatic Arts admitted African American students, and it emphasized regionalist writing, under the professors E. C. Mabie and E. P. Conkle (Wentz). Representations of African American life were encouraged, whether written by African American or white students. A Jewish student who preceded Williams at Iowa, Richard Maibaum, wrote an anti-lynching play, *The Tree*, as his 1931 master's thesis. Maibaum took the play to New York, where *The Tree* became the first anti-lynching play produced on Broadway (Atkinson). Fanny McConnell—who would later found the Negro People's Theater in Chicago, marry the author Ralph Ellison, and help edit his seminal work *Invisible Man* (Martin)—received her BA in Dramatic Art from Iowa in 1936 (Hill and Hill 76). The year after her graduation, Thomas Pawley, an African American graduate student and classmate of Williams, penned the play *Ku Klux*, about a Supreme Court nominee's Klan connections. (Justice Hugo Black's nomination to the Supreme Court by Franklin Roosevelt in 1937 was threatened by his early Klan membership and was a front-page story in the campus newspaper when Pawley and Williams were students ["Black Hints" 1].) Tom Williams, in one of his rare onstage performances, even undertook a role in the play (Pawley 67).

The Union of St. Louis Artists and Writers, an offshoot of the Communist Party composed of leftist artists and writers, constituted another formative peer group during Williams's twenties (Wixson, "Jack Conroy"). Members included the writers Clark Mills—whom Leverich deems one of the "most profound influences in [Williams's] young adult life" (336)—and Jack Conroy. Conroy, a white writer, published a proletarian literary magazine called *The Anvil*, which included work by Richard Wright and Langston Hughes (and which accepted work submitted by Williams but never published it [Hale 16]). Group members were invested in race-related activism: Conroy, for example, later collaborated with Arna Bontemps on books about African American migration from the rural South to the urban North (Wixson, *Worker-Writer* 453). The social realist painter Joe Jones, another group member, led a class of unemployed African Americans in creating a mural in the Old Courthouse that lampooned racial injustice and political corruption in St. Louis (Walker 36). Though Williams never became an official member of the group, its progressive point of view proved a strong force amid the conflicting pressures of family, community, and local and national politics that shaped his treatment of race throughout his career.

"Goat Song"

Likely written in the late 1930s, the play "Goat Song" displays evidence of several influences: the artist union's proletarianism, the Iowa writing program's emphasis on regionalism, and the time the playwright spent in New Orleans in 1938 and 1939. The manuscript consists of a one-and-a-half-page summary (whose details differ significantly from the play itself) and thirty-eight pages of playscript and revisions (including handwritten notes).

The play is set in a cabin in the Cajun country of Louisiana, where Jabe Le Grand is married to thirteen-year-old Beauty. Jabe's mother, the reader learns, died when he was born, and his father took up with a light-skinned black woman: the product of the union is the character Jacques, Jabe's half-brother of mixed race. The jealous rivalry between Jabe and Jacques has distinct racial overtones. Still living is the siblings' paternal grandmother, Granny, who is described as a "sorceress." Although she is presumably white, her "sorceress" identity and spiritual role in the community suggests connections to African or pagan roots.

Adding to the pagan mysticism of the play is the setting, which is painted as nearly primeval: "a rude cabin in the Cajun country of Louisiana. A swampy region, sparsely settled, whose chief industries are lumbering and sugarcane. The people are semi-primitive." Williams drenches the play in a version of Cajun dialect:

> JABE: Beauty—Come 'ere.
> BEAUTY: Naw.
> JABE: Come 'ere, Beauty.
> BEAUTY: (*rising with a frightened look*) Naw!
> JABE: You an' me's married, ain't we? We's married legal ain't we? You 'member what de preacher say to you. He say 'Obey dis man. He yo' husban'!' You Pappy say de same ting. He tell you go wit me, live wit me like my wife. Ain' dat wot he say, Beauty?
> BEAUTY: (*retreating carefully, the doll clutched against her*) Naw.

> JABE: You quit "nawin" me now and lissen wot I say. Jabe's yo'
> man. He's yo sweet daddy, now, ain't he?
>
> BEAUTY: Naw.

The characters' crude language matches the crude understandings of race throughout the play—some intended by the playwright, and some perhaps inadvertent. The overt racism of the characters is constructed with obviously crude language: for example, Jabe complains that if Beauty continues to withhold from him, he will "get me a nigger to live with like Pappy." Granny Le Grand insists that the father's mistress was not African American, but she warns that if Jabe takes up with a nonwhite woman, the "folks" around the area would run her off as they had "the las' one you had on the place." Despite Granny's denial, it is clear that Jabe's brother Jacques is of mixed race. Taking full advantage of his racial dominance, Jabe knocks Jacques down and locks him up with "nigger chains."

Less obviously crude is the romantic racialism used to depict the mixed-race Jacques (Crandell 342). Drunken, vulgar Jabe, who terrorizes his child-wife, breaks her doll, and shreds the pretty dress he bought her, contrasts starkly with the compassionate Jacques, who gently gives Beauty the gift of a butterfly. While Jabe is gone, Granny releases Jacques from the chains, pronounces him superior to his white half-brother, and urges him to leave the community that is bound to destroy him:

> You got to promise you go way frum this place an' don' come back. You my gran'son too. Maybe you got a li'l black blood in you veins but you good just the same. You whole lot better'n that Jabe. You go way like yo' mammy done—New Orleans or Baton Rouge—some big place like that—don' you stay here an' get you'self in trouble over that li'l yellow haired girl! It's trouble, I mean! Big trouble! I kin see it.

Jacques's compassion for Beauty develops into a love affair: when she becomes pregnant with his child, she runs away to his treehouse in the overgrown canebrake, where they live a childlike fantasy.

Williams uses broad brushstrokes in depicting character relationships to race, gender, and sexuality: the mixed-race, illegitimate brother Jacques is sensitive, idealized, in all ways superior to the white bully, Jabe. The play celebrates the naive relationship between Jacques and Beauty, which retains its innocence even when it becomes sexualized. The lovers share a joy-filled relationship, living intimately with each other and the natural world.

Their primordial paradise, however, is overtaken by primitive jealousy and uncivilized racism and revenge. When the baby is born, Beauty returns to Jabe's cabin, and Granny concocts a story to protect the girl from her jealous husband. Granny asserts that the child is a "miracle baby," claiming that a giant white goat with golden horns and stars for eyes brought Beauty the baby in the woods, announcing her as the mother of a new messiah. Jabe is initially persuaded by the old woman's mystical tone. Jacques and Beauty continue their secret nights in the treehouse until discovered by Jabe. Burning with jealousy and racial animosity, the enraged husband shoots Beauty and kills Jacques by setting his tree ablaze. In the final scene Jabe returns to his cabin, confessing the murders and begging Granny's forgiveness. He tries to justify his action to Granny, saying, "I thought she was innocent. An' even then—even then—she was runnin' out to the tree-house nights to lie with that half-nigger bastard of yours." He tells her, "She made a fool of me!"[1]

In this early work, the act of retribution leaves Jabe destroyed, not victorious, and the reader enjoys the satisfaction of seeing the bigoted white man punished for his sins. In "Goat Song" his assumed racial superiority and jealousy bring him to his knees. This ending contrasts with the more familiar early play, *Battle of Angels* (1940), in which the brutal white husband (Jabe Torrance) returns to take jealous revenge, but audiences are given little reason think justice will be served. Jabe Torrance shoots his wife and incites a mob to burn his rival, Val (who, like Jacques, also has a Cajun background, claims Native American parentage, and in some drafts is suggested to be African American passing as white). Unlike in "Goat Song," in *Battle of Angels* neither Jabe nor the white vigilantes face any form of justice.

"Goat Song" prefigures some of the themes and plot devices that Williams inserted into more complicated equations in later works. The half-brothers with mixed-race parentage appear again in the 1942 story "The Kingdom of Earth," which was written while Williams's career was still in its early stages and which went through continued transformation into dramatic versions. *Twenty-Seven Wagons Full of Cotton* and *Baby Doll* both feature a brutish white man (named Jake instead of Jabe) with a "child" wife and a rival in the form of a dark-skinned other, who, like Jacques in "Goat Song," is more playful and romantic than the loutish Jake. In both texts, the young wife (Flora or Baby Doll) relates naturally to the racial, cultural other and rejects the societally endorsed white husband. As in "Goat Song," the young wife has become pregnant by her darker-skinned lover.

"Heavenly Grass"

A fugitive, expectant couple also features in "Heavenly Grass," a libretto for a nativity-themed folk opera whose drafts bear different subtitles ("The Miracles at Granny's" and "The Song of the Turned-Out People").[2] The title "Heavenly Grass" was used later in 1946 when Williams published the "Blue Mountain Ballads," for which Paul Bowles set several of Williams's lyrics to music. The lyrics were published as a poem in the collection *In the Winter of Cities* in 1956. The folk-opera libretto predated both of those forms. According to Nicholas Moschovakis and David Roessel, Williams included it in an unpublished 1942 collection titled "Blue Mountain Blues" with a note explaining, "This collection is written primarily as lyrics for blues music or a folk opera but no music has been composed for them yet" (qtd. in Moschovakis and Roessel 236).

Putting the pieces of manuscript together, it seems that the author intended to write an updated narrative based on the biblical story of Jesus's birth, re-set in a Mississippi delta crossroads referred to as "Cinder Hill" outside of Blue Mountain. An African American Granny Woman (recalling the Granny of "Goat Song") manages a waystation. A group of "turned-out people," African American laborers laid off from "the great big syndicate plantation south of Bobo," arrive with Mary and Joseph (Joe) among them. They seek shelter for the birth of their child. Granny Woman takes them in. A marshal, preacher, and mob of vigilantes dressed in Klan garb threaten the migrant band and label Joe "uppity" when he defends the group. Though the vigilantes fire shotguns at the turned-out people, no one is hurt. When the vigilantes try to blow up the cabin, their explosion fizzles. When they try to chase Granny Woman and the holy family inside, they get an electric shock from the screen door. A divine power seems to be offering protection.

A miraculous night ensues in which Granny Woman proclaims, "The fiery black poem of God is spoken in your presence!" Time stands still and a star illuminates the place. It is "the longest and brightest night in the history of creation." The workers' previous employer announces that he is rehiring everyone, raising wages, and cutting hours. He will even turn over shares in the corporation to the workers. Granny Woman steps out resplendent in a purple gown, announcing, "Look here, you stars of heaven! This here is life beginning! Look! The Child!" The vigilantes remove their hoods, amazed by the radiant child whose very feet glow, evidence of his holiness. Granny Woman explains, "His feet took a walk in heavenly grass." As Mary and Joe prepare to leave, Joe explains, "[T]he world is full of Turned-Out People. Wherever we go we'll find our place amongst 'em." The folk opera ends with Mary singing:

> I see a cloud the shape of a goat.
> A song was always in my throat!
> I see a cloud the shape of a tree.
> The song will never let me be!
>
> I see a cloud the shape of a hand.
> [*Speaking*] I was born in the heart of a hungry land!
> I see a cloud the shape of a *fist*
> And my feet walk on through heavenly mist!

"Heavenly Grass" is a peculiar folk-style piece written in a broad dialect similar to that in "Goat Song." It contains echoes of George Gershwin's 1935 *Porgy and Bess* and the folk dramas of Paul Green. It may share characteristics of plays written by Williams's fellow students at Iowa, Thomas Pawley and Richard Maibaum, who also crafted dialect plays. As with many of Williams's unpublished texts, "Heavenly Grass" displays surprising dramaturgy and style far from the realism of his most popular work. His bold attempts at different forms such as this folk opera highlight his inclination toward expressive extremes, including the surrealism and allegory that appear in the experimental late plays.

"Heavenly Grass" situates African American characters at the center of the drama. Additional examples of the romantic racialism of Williams's early works, the characters are oppressed but noble people, presented in opposition to the dim-witted white vigilantes. Granny Woman of "Heavenly Grass" may have been drawn from Williams's childhood memories of Ozzie, his nanny. Life in the Episcopal rectory may have suggested the nativity storyline and identification of the infant Jesus as a liberator of the turned-out people.

Although religious allusions appear throughout Williams's work, "Heavenly Grass" is not merely allusive but is in fact the author's own *Second Shepherds' Play*, a retelling of the nativity story in vernacular terms. As a dramatic work of its era, it situates Williams alongside the progressive voices challenging social norms by calling out injustice and bigotry. Burdened with stereotypes and oversimplifications, however, the libretto is no more stageable today than it was in the early 1940s. The treatment of race that was too edgy and transgressive at the time is too insensitive in the twenty-first century. "Heavenly Grass" and "Goat Song" condemn overt racism but also simplistically idealize nonwhite characters. Another unpublished text, however, developed between 1939 and 1943, shows the author's emerging self-awareness of his own tendency toward romantic racialism.

"Why Did Desdemona Love the Moor?"

More nuanced and complicated in its treatment of race than either of the unpublished works discussed above, "Why Did Desdemona Love the Moor?" is the story of a Hollywood actor (named Helen in most versions, though she is Gloria in some drafts) and a writer (initially named David but later revised to Kip)[3] whose work is being adapted as a motion picture in which she is starring. The third character in this compact story is Renaldo, Helen's gay confidant. Helen is a white woman from Memphis, and Kip is African American.

Dated August 1939, the short story was initially drafted in Taos, New Mexico, where Williams had stopped to visit D. H. Lawrence's widow, Frieda. The 1939 draft of the story has a complete beginning, middle, and end, although some of its eight segments were not fully formed. Williams revised the story after the summer of 1940, expanding on and sometimes rewriting the original characters and scenes in several different ways but without pulling the pieces together into a finished whole. The revisions may have been written as late as 1943, when the playwright worked in Hollywood, since the play shows familiarity with that culture. The story exists in two manuscript versions, dated 1939 and 1943, both of which can be found in the Williams collection at the HRC in a collection of unnumbered pages. The two versions can be considered together as forming one composite story.[4]

Of significance to the revisions is the influence of a production of Shakespeare's *Othello* that was planned and staged between the 1939 version of "Desdemona" (which addressed race indirectly) and the later version (which was much more explicit on the subject). During the summer of 1940 Williams was working on *Battle of Angels* with the director Margaret Webster, who was simultaneously planning the *Othello* production with Paul Robeson. (The Webster-Robeson *Othello* finally materialized in 1942 [Swindall 76–77].) It is hard to imagine that Williams was not aware of the Webster-Robeson plans. Robeson was outspoken about problems with roles for and treatment of African Americans onstage and in film, and he was forthright about his responsibility as a representative of "the Negro race" (66). The production of *Othello*, then, was more than just another staging of Shakespeare's classic. It put a major African American actor on the Broadway stage opposite a white woman. Themes of racial difference, jealousy, and desire in *Othello* connect it to "Desdemona" and show the influence of the Webster-Robeson production.

As the title suggests, the story addresses Helen's attraction to Kip, whom she identifies as a mysterious other. In their first encounter, Helen reveals her attraction in this exchange:

> "Funny," she said, "you're not at all like a writer."
> "No? What do I look like?"
> "You're like a garage-mechanic."
> "My God!" shrieked Renaldo, looking a little bit worried from one to the other.
> The young negro's face didn't change. But she captured his eyes. They burned at her terribly whitely. Her hand unconsciously stretched across the table and picked up the dark lensed glasses and fitted them on.
> "No, but he *does*," she insisted.

> Better stop *now*. But she couldn't. The look was a chal-
> lenge to her.
>
> "He looks like one of those hairy, greasy *irresistible* men
> that climb all over your car in garages and make you feel like
> you're being *raped* by *proxy*!"

After an uncomfortable moment Kip responds, saying, "What you meant is that I am a negro." The subject of race is unapologetically established from the beginning. Kip takes his leave, but not until he explains, "I have never mixed with white people. Though sometimes people don't seem to notice my color. Still," he goes on, "I've preferred to stay with my own."

In a later scene, Helen recalls a discussion from her high school days in which the teacher had asked, "Why did Desdemona love the Moor?" The boys in the class had laughed and whispered among themselves, presumably linking Othello's race with sexual prowess. The high-school-aged Helen had offered her perspective this way:

> She loved the Moor . . . because he was dark and fatal! He had
> no patience with little things or little people! He came rushing
> into her sheltered, commonplace life like a *storm* and all the
> stupid, tiresome things were *swept before him*! In his actions he
> was *cruel* and *savage* but in his heart he was *tender*—and so she
> *loved* him, even when he suffocated her with the pillow, I think
> she *loved* him, she worshipped him like a *god*!

Despite or because of the racial tension, there is sexual chemistry between the two characters. As the playwright did in other work that featured African American characters (and characters not explicitly black but coded as such), Williams associated the black man with "savagery" (see, e.g., Crandell's tracking of "beast" associations in *Streetcar* [340–41]). The Othello that Helen imagined, however, was also tender-hearted and loving, inspiring in her the simultaneous "fear and desire" described by Morrison. Helen's Othello was also impatient with petty concerns and motivated by bigger issues—in other words, he was idealized by Helen, the romantic racialist. Her high school notion of Othello had much to do with his passion and not so much with animalistic wildness. Her Othello was not subhuman but superhuman.

After admitting her racist instincts, Helen apologizes to Kip, calling herself a "bitch" who has been hungry for "excitement—experience—*life*!"

Kip recognizes her as a woman who is "rich and soft and successful and full of a great self-pity!" He explains that his emotional resources are reserved for "his own kind of people." After a frank discussion of their racial attitudes, the starlet and the writer engage in a sexual affair that takes them to a secluded mountain cabin. Trying to understand her attraction to Kip, Helen prods him to share about himself. He holds back, coolly observing that there is too much difference between them, and it seems that the affair has no future. On the tense drive back down the mountain, Kip confesses a previous affair with a woman who "had some spaces in her that didn't have to be filled with spermatozoa." The harsh misogyny of Kip's comment, one could argue, reflects Williams's growing ability to temper romantic racialism by identifying more complex and even unattractive aspects of character. Pushed beyond her limit, Helen reacts to Kip's insensitivity by jumping out of the roadster. Startled, Kip crashes the car, setting off a rockslide. The lovers survive the avalanche, tacitly reaching an understanding in the final moments of the story:

> He called her name three times before he reached her.
> "You're not hurt?"
> "No," she answered.
> The ecstasy in her face confused him at first.
> Why was she smiling? What was this brightness for?
> And then the incommunicable thing that was in her, the thwarted tenderness that was more than passion, flooded through him undammed and he understood that this was speech beyond language.
> The love in him clenched like a fist.
> He caught her against him.
> "Helen, I've been—"
> "I know!"
> She leaned against him lightly and they moved on up the road through the golden filter of dust, separate yet together, two equal beings . . .

Williams's short story is notable for several reasons. It portrays Kip as an intellectual, urbane African American man: a successful writer with status equal to or greater than Helen's. He is not the brutish black man that Williams crafted in works like "Big Black: A Mississippi Idyll" or "Desire and the Black Masseur." The discussion of race is surprisingly self-aware, acknowledging Helen's biased preconceptions and the influence of their shared southern roots. Speaking from his own perspective, Kip addresses the discomfort he feels as a black man in the white world of Hollywood. Like Paul Robeson, he speaks about an obligation to represent "his people." Kip shows little patience with the privileged white woman's self-centered needs. The difference between them is his expansive awareness of social responsibility compared with her preoccupation with emotional need and physical desire. Helen struggles with her attraction and aversion to a black man but tries to understand it as the product of a southern upbringing. Kip recognizes the invisible wall of deep prejudice between them. The interracial couple nevertheless maintain a sexual relationship that does not depend on common racial stereotypes. In several scenes they reveal their naked bodies but not in overtly sexualized ways. On a hike up the mountain she removes her shirt. In a trailside pool, he casually bathes. They lie together in bed, not in the act of sex but in quieter moments that place skin against skin. When the story ends after the near-calamitous rockslide they come together with "the thwarted tenderness that is more than passion." They move "separate yet together." They do not have to pay a price for their interracial transgression, as would be a more typical resolution in works of this era: they suffer no explicit social punishment, and the rockslide, which could have been understood as metaphorical punishment, is deemed by Helen "an absolution." Instead of being torn apart by racial difference, they seem to find a way to coexist.

"Why Did Desdemona Love the Moor?" expands on a plot that Williams had been pursuing through several of his early plays (the character of a young woman who is attracted to a man from an unsanctioned class) and explicitly engages with themes that he will explore more covertly in later work: In *Fugitive Kind* (1937), his second play produced in St. Louis, a young woman, Glory, falls for an escaped felon, Terry Meighan, whose dangerous otherness is more attractive to her than the security of life with a safe fiancé. In *Spring Storm*, written a little later (1937–38), Heavenly is torn between two suitors: one is rich but sexless, the other a man of action with sex appeal but no money or social status. Later, in 1947, *Streetcar*'s Blanche DuBois is attracted to and repelled by the danger of Stanley Kowalski. Alexandra Del Lago from *Sweet Bird of Youth* and

Flora Goforth from *The Milk Train Doesn't Stop Here Anymore* (1963) are older versions of the Helen of "Desdemona," hungering for dangerous younger lovers. Although the later works do not depict the object of desire as a racial other as explicitly as "Desdemona" does, they share many other characteristics.

"Goat Song," "Heavenly Grass," and "Why Did Desdemona Love the Moor?" are only a sampling of revealing Williams works not published or produced during the author's lifetime. The story "His Father's House" and the short plays *Jungle; or, Walter Finds the Pearl* and *Escape* incorporate African American characters and explicitly racial themes, and the working drafts of *Battle of Angels* also include nonwhite characters and issues of race not in the published version.[5]

The relative absence of nonwhite characters in Williams's popular work need not lead the reader to assume that the playwright was unconcerned with racial matters. Awareness and study of unpublished material in which race plays a central role allows readers to recognize and reassess the ways Williams wrestled with the topic and how his approaches evolved. Viewed from the twenty-first century, Williams's treatment of racial issues can seem clumsy, limited, and insensitive. Like Helen in "Desdemona," Williams seems to have been fascinated by the racial other in complex, often sympathetic ways but also conditioned to reduce that other to a stereotype. And yet, while the three early works examined here do use nonwhite characters as stereotypical functionaries, the characters' central placement also shows Williams attempting in various (successful and unsuccessful) ways to challenge the racism of his era. In "Goat Song" the mixed-race brother, Jacques, is the romantic hero. In "Heavenly Grass," Mary and Joe lead an African American religious pageant and are figured as bringing the messiah into the world. In "Why Did Desdemona Love the Moor?" Kip is a mature artist and lover, capable of pointing out to well-meaning white audiences their own unconscious racism. These works are the beginnings of Williams's career-long efforts to empathize with the other—his perpetual positioning of himself alongside African American, Mexican, female, gay, mentally fragile, and socially outcast characters, embracing their otherness, struggling with simultaneous impulses to stereotype and to imagine them instead as people with feeling, thought, and motivation. In its approaches to race, Williams's artistic output was dangerous in his time, more so than is sometimes perceived today, and examining the unpublished works proves valuable to our understanding of the canonical plays and of his entire body of work.

Notes

[1] In the summary of "Goat Song," the names are different from the dialogue pages. Jabe is "Boss Karle." Beauty is "Pearl." Jacques is "Guy," an Irish youth who is "a poet or an artist escaping from the outside world." In this summary, the people of the community are temporarily convinced that the child is the "new messiah," but when the secret is revealed they rise up to take out their wrath on Pearl. Boss Karle "lies in a drunken stupor on the floor," and the old woman with the child in her arms "wanders off into the swamp to find the large white goat which she hears singing in the moonlight." These plot details differ significantly from the dramatic version that exists in manuscript in the Williams materials at HRC.

[2] "Heavenly Grass" is on file in the HRC. The file includes eighty-eight unnumbered and mostly undated pages. The material offers several versions of scenes and characters. As a libretto for a folk opera, it contains much text written in rhyming verse or as material for recitative. Gilbert Debusscher discusses this work in the article "Tennessee Williams's Black Nativity: An Unpublished Libretto."

[3] In the 1939 version, the writer character is named David and the starlet is Helen. In the revisions, the writer is Kip and the actor is sometimes called Gloria. The writer character's name change from "David" to "Kip" is no doubt related to Williams's affair with the dancer Kip Kiernan in Provincetown in summer 1940. I have chosen to use the names Kip and Helen in this essay.

[4] The file "Why Did Desdemona Love the Moor?" in the HRC includes a twenty-two-page version of the story that concludes with the following typed information:

> Tennessee Williams
>
> Taos, New Mexico
>
> August, 1939

There are forty-nine additional pages of revisions, a few in dramatic dialogue with the alternative title "The Bitch." In this essay, quotations and references to plot, character, and themes are drawn from my edited version of "Why Did Desdemona Love the Moor?" (forthcoming in the *Tennessee Williams Annual Review*), a composite text that incorporates the twenty-two-page version (1939) and the additional unnumbered pages (1943). Sasser's essay "Unraveling the 'Desdemona Thing' in Tennessee Williams," published in the 2016 *Tennessee Williams Annual Review*, discusses the story as it exists in its original fragmented form at the HRC.

⁵ Unpublished material from *Battle of Angels* can be found in the Williams collections at HRC and Harvard. Margaret Webster's promptbook for the production is in the Library of Congress. Additional material is in the Erwin Piscator collection at Southern Illinois University Special Collections Research Center. Other resources on the multiple versions of the play can be found in Claudia Wilsch Case's essay "Inventing Tennessee Williams: The Theatre Guild and His First Professional Production" and Robert Bray's "*Battle of Angels* and *Orpheus Descending.*"

Works Cited

Atkinson, J. Brooks. Review of *The Tree*. *New York Times*, 13 Apr. 1934, p. 23.

Bigsby, C. W. E. *Modern American Drama, 1945–2000*. Cambridge UP, 2000.

"Black Hints at Radio Reply to KKK Charge." *Daily Iowan*, 30 Sept. 1937.

Bray, Robert. "*Battle of Angels* and *Orpheus Descending.*" *Tennessee Williams: A Guide to Research and Performance*, edited by Philip C. Kolin, Greenwood Press, 1998, pp. 22–33.

Brewer, Mary F. *Staging Whiteness*. Wesleyan UP, 2005.

Case, Claudia Wilsch. "Inventing Tennessee Williams: The Theatre Guild and His First Professional Production." *Tennessee Williams Annual Review*, vol. 8, 2006, pp. 51–71.

Crandell, George W. "Misrepresentation and Miscegenation: Reading the Racialized Discourse of Tennessee Williams's *A Streetcar Named Desire.*" *Modern Drama*, vol. 40, no. 3, 1997, pp. 337–46.

Debusscher, Gilbert. "Tennessee Williams's Black Nativity: An Unpublished Libretto." *Costerus: American Literature in Belgium*, vol. 66, Rodopi, 1988, pp. 127–33.

Gilmour, Austin. "Lynching in America." *Vanity Fair*, vol. 42, June 1935. *Vanity Fair: The Complete Archive*, stag-archive.vanityfair.com/article/1935/06/01/lynching-in-america. Accessed 13 Dec. 2018.

Hale, Allean. "Early Williams: The Making of a Playwright." *The Cambridge Companion to Tennessee Williams*, edited by Matthew C. Roudané, Cambridge UP, 1977, pp. 11–28.

Heathcott, Joseph. "Black Archipelago: Politics and Civic Life in the Jim Crow City." *Journal of Social History*, vol. 38, no. 3, 2005, pp. 705–36.

Hill, Lena M., and Michael D. Hill, editors. *Invisible Hawkeyes: African Americans at the University of Iowa during the Long Civil Rights Era*. U of Iowa P, 2016.

Kolin, Philip C. "Race." *The Tennessee Williams Encyclopedia*, edited by Kolin, Greenwood Press, 2004, pp. 204–08.

Leverich, Lyle. *Tom: The Unknown Tennessee Williams*. Crown Publishers, 1995.

Martin, Douglas. "Fanny Ellison, 93, Dies; Helped Husband Edit 'Invisible Man.'" *New York Times*, 1 Dec. 2005, www.nytimes.com/2005/12/01/arts/fanny-ellison-93-dies-helped-husband-edit-invisible-man.html.

Miller, Arthur. *Timebends: A Life*. Grove Press, 1987.

Moschovakis, Nicholas, and David Roessel, editors. *The Collected Poems of Tennessee Williams*. New Directions, 2002.

"Negro Slayer of Teacher Lynched at Maryville, Mo.; Burned with Schoolhouse." *St. Louis Post-Dispatch*, 12 Jan. 1931, p. 1.

Pawley, Thomas D. "Experimental Theatre Seminar; or, The Basic Training of Tennessee Williams: A Memoir." *The Iowa Review*, vol. 19, no. 1, 1989, pp. 64–76.

Sasser, M. Tyler. "Unraveling the 'Desdemona Thing' in Tennessee Williams." *Tennessee Williams Annual Review*, vol. 15, 2016, pp. 147–63.

Swindall, Lindsey R. *The Politics of Paul Robeson's* Othello. UP of Mississippi, 2011.

Thompson, Julius E. *Lynchings in Mississippi: A History, 1865–1965*. McFarland, 2007.

Tischler, Nancy M. "Tennessee Williams's South: A Portrait of a Mid-Twentieth-Century American Culture." *Tennessee Williams Literary Journal*, vol. 3, no. 2, Fall 1995, pp. 45–55.

Walker, Andrew, general editor. *Joe Jones: Radical Painter of the American Scene*. Saint Louis Art Museum / Washington Press, 2010.

Wentz, John C. "American Regional Drama, 1920–40: Frustration and Fulfillment." *Modern Drama*, vol. 6, no. 3, 1963, pp. 286–93.

Williams, Tennessee. Baby Doll *and* Tiger Tail. New Directions, 1991.

———. *Battle of Angels*. Williams, *Theatre*, vol. 1, pp. 1–122.

———. "Big Black: A Mississippi Idyll." *Collected Stories*, New Directions, 1985, pp. 26–31.

———. "Desire and the Black Masseur." *Collected Stories*, New Directions, 1985, pp. 205–12.

———. *Escape*. Mister Paradise *and Other One-Act Plays by Tennessee Williams*, edited with notes by Nicholas Moschovakis and David Roessel, New Directions, 2005, pp. 37–43.

———. *Fugitive Kind*. Edited by Allean Hale, New Directions, 2001.

———. "Goat Song." Tennessee Williams Collection, Harry Ransom Center, U of Texas, Austin, box 17, folder 11.

———. "Heavenly Grass; or, The Miracles at Granny's; or, The Song of the Turned-Out People." Tennessee Williams Collection, Harry Ransom Center, U of Texas, Austin, box 18, folder 8.

———. "His Father's House." Edited by Robert Bray, *Tennessee Williams Annual Review*, vol. 7, 2005, pp. 5–13.

———. *In the Winter of Cities*. New Directions, 1956.

———. "'Jungle; or, Walter Finds the Pearl': A Previously Unpublished One-Act Play by Tennessee Williams." *Resources for American Literary Study*, vol. 32, June 2009, pp. 241–66.

———. *Kingdom of Earth*. Williams, *Theatre*, vol. 5, pp. 121–214.

———. *The Last of My Solid Gold Watches*. Williams, *Theatre*, vol. 6, pp. 93–105.

——. *Memoirs.* Doubleday, 1975.

——. *Not about Nightingales.* New Directions, 1998.

——. *Orpheus Descending.* Williams, *Theatre,* vol. 3, pp. 217–342.

——. *Spring Storm.* Edited by Dan Isaac, New Directions, 1999.

——. *A Streetcar Named Desire.* Williams, *Theatre,* vol. 1, pp. 239–419.

——. *The Theatre of Tennessee Williams.* New Directions, 1971–92. 8 vols.

——. "Why Did Desdemona Love the Moor?" Tennessee Williams Collection, Harry Ransom Center, U of Texas, Austin, box 51, folder 15. Edited by Tom Mitchell, forthcoming in the *Tennessee Williams Annual Review.*

Wixson, Douglas. "Jack Conroy and the East St. Louis Toughs." *New Letters,* vol. 57, no. 4, 1991, pp. 29–57.

——. *Worker-Writer in America: Jack Conroy and the Tradition of Midwestern Literary Radicalism, 1898–1990.* U of Illinois P, 1993.

Painting His Nudes: Tennessee Williams's Homoerotic Art

====================================*Michael S. D. Hooper*

> When I had finished reading, the good professor's eyes had a
> glassy look as though he had drifted into a state of trance. There
> was a long and all but unendurable silence. Everyone seemed
> more or less embarrassed. At last the professor pushed back
> his chair, thus dismissing the seminar, and remarked casually
> and kindly, "Well, we all have to paint our nudes!" (Williams,
> "Past" 80)

Tennessee Williams's rather theatrical account in 1957 of the reaction of his playwriting professor E. C. Mabie to the reading of his play *Spring Storm* (1938) has been roundly dismissed by Dan Isaac as "a marvelous piece of comic mythic memory" (xv). Written down two decades after the purported event, Williams's (allegedly) revisionist characterization of his early work may have been intended to suggest the origins of his prurience, the sensationalism that would give him public notoriety from *A Streetcar Named Desire* (1947) onward. Alternatively, perhaps he wanted to reinforce the idea that his was an inauspicious start to becoming a successful dramatist, one not helped by a professor who favored political writing and who appeared to have opposed Williams personally.[1] Isaac, though, qualifies his comment by citing a passage in an earlier version of the play, entitled *April Is the Cruelest Month*, that could have elicited such a comment from Mabie. In it, the female protagonist, Helen (Heavenly in *Spring Storm*) Critchfield, slips out of her dress and stands in "*statue-like form*" (qtd. in Isaac xvi), illuminated by lightning, before her would-be lover, Arthur Shannon.

Above all, the comment seems prescient: if Williams's 1957 invention, it anticipates the nude figures he would paint in the 1970s, the subject of this essay—and if indeed Mabie's comment in the 1930s, it anticipates not only the later paintings but also the nudes that Williams would create on stage and in his stories, characters like Stanley Kowalski, Brick Pollitt, and Flora Goforth, who undress or appear semi-clothed and who invite our gaze. Additionally, the remark—and the playwright's choice to include it in his 1957 essay—draws attention to Williams's highly visual dramaturgy. Before we are shown Helen's sculpted silhouette, her dress falls in a pictorial *"white cascade round her feet"* (qtd. in Isaac xvi), and in countless plays Williams paints his scenes (through introductions and stage directions), refers to famous painters and their works, or does both. Most memorably, perhaps, he alludes to Vincent van Gogh's *Night Café* in the *"lurid nocturnal brilliance"* necessary for the poker night in *A Streetcar Named Desire* (286). But the pastel-colored tablecloth on which a collection of articles is arranged *"as if for a painter's still-life"* in *Will Mr. Merriwether Return from Memphis?* (1969) is not an insignificant touch in a work that features the apparition of van Gogh (230); and the Picassoesque dislocation of the porch and yard indicated in the set design for *The Gnädiges Fräulein* (1966) is a shortcut to the distorted values of that play's world.[2] These are just some examples of Williams's widespread practice of planning "his sets, costumes, and lighting with a painter's eye" (Boxill 24), of employing a visual aesthetic in which images trump words.

Painters, famous or wholly fictional, feature as significant characters in all forms of Williams's writing, not just the drama that is his primary legacy. *The Holy Family*, an incomplete and unperformed play that he was working on at roughly the same time as *April Is the Cruelest Month*, is about van Gogh and "an artist's relations to society—not one artist but all" (*Selected Letters* 116). "The Dangerous Painters," a poem included in the volume *In the Winter of Cities* (1954), describes the revolutionary potential of artists from whose canvases "something is always springing, barely leashed" (40). These are mad creators that anticipate the spray-gun artists of Williams's later plays, *The Day on Which a Man Dies* (1960) and *In the Bar of a Tokyo Hotel* (1969). *Moise and the World of Reason*, Williams's postmodern novel of 1975, has a cast of jealous and unstable painters, not least the title character, whose diminishing reason coincides with the depletion of her artistic materials.

Like his writers, Williams's painters are oddballs, romanticized rebels, misunderstood or underappreciated vagabonds on the fringes of society, escaping bourgeois respectability or just too impoverished to think beyond a day-to-day existence. In the early plays, we encounter Jim holed up in his leaky garret in *The Magic Tower* (1936) and Vee Talbot in *Battle of Angels* (1940), a mystic whose "very peculiar pictures" nonetheless suggest the heightened aestheticism of one who can "paint a thing the way that it strikes me instead of always the way that it actually is" (29, 61). Later, there is Hannah Jelkes in *The Night of the Iguana* (1961), the quick-sketch artist with "a proud person's hope of acceptance when it is desperately needed," who finds herself in her own room with a leaky roof, on the Costa Verde (278). Later still, there is the tubercular and predatory Nightingale in *Vieux Carré* (1977), a quick-sketch artist, too, but one who prostitutes his talent for French Quarter tourists. Unsurprisingly, given the importance Williams places on visual art, all comment on the nature of their work and their position in society.

In addition, Williams's nonfiction explains the transformative power of art, the importance of imagery in his drama, and the critical role played by painters. In his essay "The Timeless World of a Play" (1951), for instance, he compares the ability of the dramatist to create a "feeling of depth and significance" through the "*arrest of time*" (59) to the talent of a sculptor in giving the human form "a purity, a beauty, which would not be possible in a living mobile form" (60). In "An Appreciation of Hans Hofmann" (1948), he lauds the abstract expressionist of his title as the natural successor of van Gogh and Picasso, as an artist whose "[p]ure light, pure color," and "pure design of pure vision" may give us sufficient faith to survive in a world where truth, compassion, and reason have been exiled (198).[3] In *Memoirs* (1975), it is, he says, the "fine painter," and not usually the writer, who can create for us "his moments of intensely perceptive being" (250).

The elevation of the painter over the writer is perhaps a reason, aside from the simple pleasure it brought, why Williams dabbled in art himself. Without presuming to be a "fine painter," he explored color and texture studiously and was happy to take instruction from the friends he cultivated to share his enthusiasm. Thus, Williams's understanding of how his dramatic scenes were achieved, their origins in images and not words, and the parallels that could be drawn with the techniques of famous artists, was complemented by his own painterly activity. In turn, as Williams's paintings become better known—they are appearing in exhibitions and have belatedly attracted the interest of scholars—we can appreciate the ways in which they take up the ideas and themes of his writing, or even attempt to recreate its characters.[4] More specifically, Williams literally painted nudes, not gratuitously or simply for gratification but to visualize and unpick the instabilities of his personal and professional lives. Rarely just pornography, these works address his preoccupation with three distinct but overlapping subjects: androgyny, fears about the essential loneliness of the human condition, and the affirmative power and iconography of Christianity. At their best and most intriguing, the paintings are themselves dramas—cryptically revealing and intertextual.

The Seventies

"If you missed the sixties, Bird, God knows what
you are going to do with the seventies."
—Gore Vidal, "Some Memories of the Glorious Bird and an Earlier Self"

"My God, an exhibition of realistic portraits just when
my non-portraits are catching on!"
—Tennessee Williams, *Moise and the World of Reason*

The sixties, a blurry decade of professional failure, personal loss, alcoholism, and addiction to prescription drugs, ended in acrimony for Williams. "[L]iving under a demented state of siege" (Lahr 497), he was forcibly committed, at the instigation of his brother, Dakin, to the psychiatric ward of Barnes Hospital in St. Louis in 1969—a life-saving act, one that Williams, though bitter in its aftermath, would slot into his personal mythology. The seventies, though promising a fresh start, brought instead more of the same, the playwright's public appearances still an embarrassment despite a greater lucidity from no longer having the protection of "an impermeable drug-induced bubble" (Bak, *Tennessee* 211). Away from the spotlight, he could enjoy the partial seclusion of 1431 Duncan Street, his Key West residence, and the relaxation afforded by painting. It has been assumed that he took up the activity when his writing was most heavily criticized and, consequently, when he was depressed: the artist Michael Garady, for example, characterizes Williams as engaging in painting "as a second profession. It started around the 60s when his career as a playwright had a bit of a dip." Painting, in other words, is presumed to be a hobby (not quite the "profession" Garady grandly terms it) that functioned as a pick-me-up, one that could be kept from formal appraisal.

In truth, however, Williams had drawn or painted most of his life. Doodles filled his notebooks; landscapes, still lifes, and portraits of anonymous performers were some of the subjects of his middle years. In the final phase of his life, his greater productivity encompassed portraits of lovers, actors, unnamed men and women, and treatments of, or responses to, literary works, both his own and those of others. On completion, the paintings were mainly gifted to friends. They were not seen as a serious venture—at least, not by their creator—or as part of an artistic portfolio that already included the writing for which Williams had increasingly become known. The works were not formally cataloged at the time, and, given that some are still in private hands, the task of identifying and accurately dating them all seems difficult, if not impossible, today. The information that is available, however, reveals that Williams's prolific period in the seventies is characterized by a more consistently figurative approach than was used in the works that came before and after. Men and women, but especially men, partially clad or naked, populate his canvases in greater numbers, creating what would appear to be the biggest subset of paintings.

Figurative Art and the Homoerotic Tradition

In *Memoirs*, Williams makes the somewhat extraordinary claim that painters and sculptors have created a greater tactility through their work than is possible through actual touch: "And those who painted and sculpted the sensuous and the sensual of naked life in its moments of glory made them palpable to you as we can never feel with our fingertips and the erogenous parts of our flesh" (250). This faith in visual artists' creative power in representing "the sensual of naked life," entirely consistent with his appreciation of painters as the purest communicators of human experience, probably motivated Williams to explore and improve his understanding of the human body. Yet, given his commitment to plastic art, this effort would not be undertaken with the aim of anatomical exactitude. Williams realized the limitations of verisimilitude, of a slavish dependence on realism; truth could be got at another way—through suggestion, mood, and perspective. While he eschewed more experimental forms for his painting, possibly out of inexperience and a lack of confidence, color and the texture of his materials invariably seem more important than the complete fidelity of lines, dimensionality, and artistic depth.

At the start of the 1970s, his subject matter, if not his technique, was in tune with a movement away from the hitherto dominant abstract expressionism toward more figurative painting. As early as 1959, artists and critics alike had championed a revival of more naturalistic techniques to paint nudes, albeit in ways that challenged and parodied the depictions of reclining figures in traditional art of the nineteenth-century and earlier. The US painter Philip Pearlstein (1924–), whose cropped nudes seem to owe much to photography, became their unofficial spokesman when he wrote his attack on abstract expressionism in 1962, "Figure Paintings Today Are Not Made in Heaven." And yet Pearlstein was also questioning those artists already engaged in figurative painting (such as Larry Rivers [1923–2002]), whom he deemed "illusionists" creating "psychological overtones" (39) that paralleled the psychological realism and modernism of novelists. For Pearlstein, true figurative painters had to acknowledge the progress represented in expressionism and understand that the nude is "a fascinating kaleidoscope of forms" (52), an ever-shifting subject of which the artist can only hope to paint one aspect or experience.

It seems unlikely that Tennessee Williams's paintings of the seventies were directly influenced by these debates, though it is worth noting that in creating the artist characters central to *The Day on Which a Man Dies* and *In the Bar of a Tokyo Hotel*, the playwright was demonstrating interest in abstract expressionists—particularly Jackson Pollock—at a time when their supremacy was being challenged. For, in truth, the particular vagaries of fashion mattered less to Williams than his fascination with the tormented painter or writer, beginning with his early interest in unstable artists like Vincent van Gogh—artists whose work is all-consuming, whose edginess and fear of failure and refusal to cater to artistic fashion hasten them to self-destruction. (Consciously or not, Williams was foretelling his own future in creating these characters: theatrical fashion would eventually contribute to his own transformation into a tortured figure.) Also vital to Williams the writer was the logical extension of his own philosophy of art. As Sophie Maruéjouls-Koch explains, Williams's plastic theater after 1961 had developed to a point where its experimentalism closely mirrored Pollock's work. Both artists were concerned with collapsing the normal boundary between life and art, replacing it with a "maze of representa-tions," "a labyrinth of masks" (45), and making little distinction between content and form. More specifically, "[l]ike Pollock, who juxtaposed layers of paint upon his canvases, Williams superimposed levels of theatricality in his late plays to create the sense of confusion that arises when all notions of limits vanish" (40).

Consistent with both this experimentation and their unstable charac-ters, Williams's Pollockian painters, Man in *The Day on Which a Man Dies* and Mark Conley in *In the Bar of a Tokyo Hotel*, achieve their effects with the apparently impersonal and haphazard spray gun, a tool very different from the conventional brush used by Williams to apply his oil and acrylic paints. But while Williams chose more traditional techniques and forms for his own paintings—perhaps only too conscious that he had not served an artistic apprenticeship—some of his lines and geometrical shapes are consistent with the set designs of his radical late plays. Decluttering the acting areas in these dramas, Williams uses simple, unobtrusive props that "make for a sterile space" conducive to the exploration of "the psycho-logical realities which are the true subjects of his expressionist creations" (Smith Ruckel 86). Terri Smith Ruckel notes, for example, how the unfussy canvases of some of Williams's paintings resemble the lines of the bar and the circle of the table at which Mark's wife, Miriam, sits in *In the Bar of a Tokyo Hotel*. Furthermore, *Many Moons Ago* (1980), *The Faith of Gatsby's Last Summer* (c. 1975), and *On ne peut pas comprendre toujours* (sic) (1980) are just three examples of paintings where, as in the play, a man and a woman seem to vie for the central space but are really connected through "the same illusion of line and shape" (88). Light and splashes of color also create a commonality of purpose, and we should not forget Williams's theory of plastic space: the simple idea, as expounded by Louise in *Will*

Mr. Merriwether Return from Memphis?, that gaps between objects, too frequently ignored, actually "give to the painting its composition" (276). Viewed together, then, Williams's paintings and those of the abstract expressionists initially seem worlds apart; connected via the concerns of the late plays, they are much closer, and Williams's interest in a figure like Pollock extends beyond mere identification with a tormented artist.

Given Williams's knowledge of painters and their relation to artistic trends, one might expect the playwright's paintings to show visual consistency with the work of his contemporaries, but just as it is difficult to connect Williams's writing after 1970 with any literary movement, it is hard to view his paintings as part of a homoerotic tradition in the United States. Twentieth-century US painters like Paul Cadmus (1904–99) and Marsden Hartley (1877–1943) approached some of their subjects with the same indirection that Williams employed in his plays—a visual coding that parallels the queer vocabulary of the closeted dramatist. Coded paintings could still court public controversy and censorship, however, Cadmus's *The Fleet's In!* (1934) being a notorious case.[5] Not surprisingly, more-explicit work was often withheld from the public, by collectors or by the artists themselves: Charles Demuth (1883–1935), for example, likely never intended public exhibition for his 1930s series of watercolors depicting sailors.[6] Williams did not push his own paintings into the public domain, even given the different social climate of the 1970s and even though, unlike Cadmus's and Demuth's scenes of the waterfront and Turkish baths, his work avoids the depiction of lewd physical contact and scenes typically associated with male intimacy. Indeed, the mood of Williams's art seems closer to that of a British import: David Hockney (1937–), who settled in Los Angeles in 1964. Hockney's homoerotic swimming pool and shower paintings of the 1960s, expressive of the utopia the artist sought after reading John Rechy's influential 1963 novel *City of Night* and viewing images from the magazine *Physique Pictorial*, document the vacuity of modern life through men who, like some of Williams's archetypal subjects, are "preoccupied figures who spend their days bathing without joy, curiously lonely" (Ristić 287). Ultimately, however, Williams was closer to twentieth-century visual artists as a dramatist than as a painter.

Hunting Youth

> The mature playwright he had become, now in decline, could reminisce on
> happier times as he painted young naked men who reminded him of an
> idealistic period when he was something of a poetic athlete, if not a sexual one.
> —William Plumley, "Tennessee Williams's Graphic Art: 'Two on a Party'"

The precise reason for the shift in Williams's artistic focus during this period is unclear. The Stonewall riots of 1969 generated a wave of optimism and pride that quickly led to the formation of the Gay Liberation Front, but it would be some while before this movement fully impacted the individual lives of nonactivists. The paintings, in themselves no proof of Williams's homosexuality, did not constitute any kind of public expression, and thus there would have been no public pressure on him to account for his choice of subject. Williams had always taken care in the distribution of his more explicitly homoerotic short stories, requesting that they not be openly displayed in St. Louis (where his mother might see them) and seeking an agreement with his publisher, New Directions, that they be issued in a private edition. However, no such caution seems to have been necessary with the paintings, as many who received them were probably already cognizant of Williams's sexuality. Goaded into coming out publicly on *The David Frost Show* in 1970, Williams had, in theory, a platform for portraying homosexuality more freely, but did his having this option really affect his painting?

Williams's choice of subject was probably subconsciously influenced by both the spirit of Stonewall and his personal circumstances. He painted men that he desired, or at least found aesthetically pleasing, in the knowledge that his sexuality was now transparent and with a sense that gay politics were finally gaining a foothold. But a more tangible reason for Williams's choice of subject was simply circumstantial: the availability of willing models. While living at his Duncan Street address in Key West, he (perhaps through some combination of his fame and the bohemian setting) seems to have attracted young men, casual callers over and above a succession of private secretaries, who were prepared to pose for him. The individual portraits that resulted, or that were inspired by the sitters, tend to suggest the men's availability. Passive rather than provocative figures, they are not conventionally idealized: they have slim but ordinary torsos that seem to defy stereotypical musculature. In paintings like *Citizen of World III: Set for Target Practise* (1970s), *Mister Paradise* (n.d.), and *La Langue Perdue* (n.d.), the subjects have a spiritual quality. They sit in peacock chairs, the fantail backs of which create aureoles and which have radial lines reminiscent of arrows piercing St. Sebastian, admittedly a conventional homoerotic icon. Moreover, the titles of these works hint at the model's being physically or personally appreciated by the artist, by implication configured as a hunter or the discoverer of true male desire and friendship. Too, Williams's somewhat adolescent facture, especially noticeable in these compositions, almost suggests his guilty pleasure in subjects that reduce him to an infatuated schoolboy.

Approaching sixty at the start of the decade, Williams no doubt found youthful company a convenient means of transporting himself back to less troubled times, as William Plumley indicates in the epigraph above. Deeper still, youth could hold at bay the real horrors of aging that Williams had, thus far, only glimpsed: physical degeneration and the specter of institutionalization, fears that would emerge in late one-act plays like *The Frosted Glass Coffin* (1970), *Lifeboat Drill* (1979), and *This Is the Peaceable Kingdom* (1980), as well as the full-length *A House Not Meant to Stand* (1981). An antidote to brooding on age, painting had the additional consolation of being free from public scrutiny and therefore a refuge. Williams could take up his paintbrush in the knowledge that his visual art would escape the sometimes vitriolic and homophobic criticism that was so demoralizing.

Androgyne

> With a boy who has the androgynous quality in spirit,
> like a poet, the thing is more spiritual.
> —Tennessee Williams, in an interview with C. Robert Jennings (1973)

Both Smith Ruckel and Maruéjouls-Koch emphasize the underlying harmony of Williams's oeuvre, Maruéjouls-Koch going further by linking this overall harmony to the playwright's interest in androgyny. Miriam and Mark in *Tokyo Hotel* are, for example, the feminine and masculine parts of one person riven apart, not completely separate entities feuding. They, like Clare and Felice in *Out Cry* (1971), or One and Two, the characters in *I Can't Imagine Tomorrow* (1970), are, to some extent, interchangeable, seeking Williams's "dream of a primordial self" (Maruéjouls-Koch 33)—a paradoxically desired and dreaded vision of androgynous unity that will never come to pass. In "Tennessee Williams and Jackson Pollock: The Art of Crossing the Line," Maruéjouls-Koch connects Williams's impetus with Pollock's vision via certain totemic figures that she discerns in paintings such as Pollock's *Male and Female* (1942–43) and in plays such as *Out Cry* and *The Gnädiges Fräulein*. The essay does not extend the link further to include Williams's painting, but her comments about androgyny in the late plays, combined with Smith Ruckel's observations on the similar techniques employed in both the plays and paintings, are helpful when we move beyond Williams's portraits of individual men. Granted, some of these single figures almost seem to promote a form of androgynous beauty in themselves, men being given fuller, rosier lips, long hair, and sloping shoulders. *Citizen of World III* is of this type, but we can even go back to a painting of an unidentified figure from 1947 to see the process in reverse: a woman with shoulder-length hair, whose heavy-set features appear very masculine. However, the painting that most obviously seems to under-line Maruéjouls-Koch's point and exemplify Williams's comments about androgyny in the seventies is *Les Etrangers Amoureuses* (1970s) (fig. 1).

Two men occupy the center of this composition, one standing and the other seated. The standing figure, seen only in profile, has the feminine features mentioned above and contrasts starkly with the seated figure, who sits back with a defiant male posture, exposing a large, flaccid penis that commands the viewer's attention. The standing figure is unquestionably a man—we have a sidelong glimpse of his penis and testicles—but he seems in many ways the opposite of his counterpart, a point reinforced by a pencil line that separates them. It is not uncommon for Williams to leave such lines—part of his initial sketching—in the final painting, but the effect here is to reinforce the dissimilarities between the two figures, to underscore their physical distance, even though they touch at one point, where the line disappears. The men, then, are divided, as if into sepa-rate paintings that have been joined together, but are also so close that they could be two versions of the male lover, one feminized and the other hypermasculine.

Fig. 1. *Les Etrangers Amoureuses* (1970s), by Tennessee Williams. Courtesy Key West Art and Historical Society, 2018.33.0082.

This central tension—a dramatic one between intimacy and separation—is captured in Williams's title: the men are, or have been, lovers but are now estranged. Their alienation from each other has left them looking off in different directions, apparently irreconcilable but physically close enough to intimate that this breach may be only temporary. The pastoral background of the painting heightens the tension, denying the lovers the privacy and intimacy normally afforded by a bedroom. And yet the mass of green foliage that surrounds the bathing platforms on which the men stand and sit creates a secluded spot in which, as their nudity signals, they can be open with each other. The innocent joy of sunbathing or swimming naked, free from censure, captured in famous paintings like Thomas Eakins's groundbreaking *Swimming* (1885, later titled *The Swimming Hole*), is noticeably absent, the only sign of relaxation other than the men's nakedness being the glass the standing figure holds at the height of his bent knee. Instead, the men seem to have been separately placed in their surroundings, a point suggested by Williams's flattened perspective. By making the bathing platforms on which they stand and sit of different heights, he forces the figures onto the same plane and creates an optical impossibility, one not immediately noticed because so much of the painting's background is ill-defined. Manipulating the figures in this way, creating a forced togetherness, can be read as underlining the conflict between the less threatening, androgynous male and the übermasculine alternative, or as the evolution of one from the other.[7] More obviously, though, the arrangement tells of the deep-seated loneliness within relationships, the lingering unhappiness behind public togetherness. Williams explored this relationship disconnect dramatically (e.g., *Cat on a Hot Tin Roof*'s Brick and Maggie, who share a metaphorical cage), though not, even post-Stonewall, within homosexual relationships.

Loneliness

Disconnectedness between men and women features in several of the paintings of this period, regardless of the proximity or spatial distance on the canvas. The crowded central area of *Nus* (1972), for example, cannot mask the awkwardness of its three naked figures, two of whom, tellingly, have their faces turned away from the viewer; and in *The Tidings Brought to Mary at Far Rockaway* (1975), a painting I will consider at greater length later, the figures pose stiltedly in their separate spaces, as if surprised to be discovered together. Objects bisect the canvases and create division much as the pencil guideline does in *Les Etrangers Amoureuses*. Vertical lines of the bed and table in *Sulla Terrazza della Signora Stone* (1970s) separate Mrs. Stone from her lover, Paolo, and, in the most autobiographical of these compositions, *On ne peut pas comprendre toujours*, Williams splices the canvas with an overarching tree that almost acts as an intermediary between two seated figures: Williams and his mother.

In general, Williams tends to explore loneliness through paintings of grouped figures rather than individuals, and thus his painting *Le Solitaire* (1976), which captures the isolation of a single figure, stands out (fig. 2). Also atypical in terms of its color, tone, and setting, the work nevertheless seems to present a coda to Williams's art of this period, and indeed to express a wider aesthetic that echoes the perennial themes of his writing. Looked at autobiographically, it suggests, perhaps more than any other painting, that Williams's attempts to surround himself with people (both his regular hangers-on and those with the proverbial kindness of strangers) and to be more open about himself publicly have, paradoxically, left him more alone than ever. This isolation was partly his own fault in that, at the start of the decade, Williams severed connections with his paid companion-secretary, Bill Glavin, and his longtime literary agent, Audrey Wood, but the deaths of friends like Jane Bowles and Anna Magnani in 1973 compounded the lingering gloom from the death of Frank Merlo in 1963. As Henry Faulkner, an eccentric painter friend, observed in an *Esquire*

Fig. 2. *Le Solitaire* (1976), by Tennessee Williams. Courtesy Key West Art and Historical Society, 2018.33.0083.

interview with Donald Newlove in 1969, "Tennessee is the most melancholy man on God's green earth. [. . .] Every morning he gets crouched right there at the starting line, ready to run to these people in his mind. It's utter loneliness" (qtd. in House 219–20).

Le Solitaire features an urban setting at night (the place and the time of day both unusual choices for Williams). Blackness engulfs the canvas: the sky is dark, apart from specks of white representing stars and a moon that, together, create a small pool of light at the foot of a palm tree; the ground is black, as is the figure in the foreground with his back to us. The naked or nearly naked figure (it is difficult to determine whether or not he is wearing pants) is merely a silhouette outlined in white. Again, this outline is created by the light of the moon. The man appears to be moving toward the palm tree and some bluish hills behind it, yet, on either side, two similarly proportioned red buildings start to converge toward a point that is either just in front of the tree, blocking the figure's access to it, or exactly at the tree, where the tree—and perhaps the man too—would be crushed between them. The implied point of convergence suggests both the possibility that he will not make the apparently short distance that remains and the fear that the figure will not be able to extricate himself from the constrictive urban sprawl that oppresses him (as it did the artist). Also, the placement of the man's hands on his hips suggests that he is not walking but is contemplating his journey and future from a stationary position.

The palm tree, in Christianity a symbol of triumph, peace, and eternal life associated with Christ's entrance into Jerusalem, appears, then, to be a goal he has yet to achieve, one that lies somewhere beyond the crushing metropolis, the city that has become synonymous with Williams's personal breakdown and the critical post-mortem performed on his late plays that largely precipitated it. "Le solitaire," or the loner, is both the man and the artist seeking consolation and recuperation. He is the dramatist searching out the softer hues of his painting, the work that will be less savagely evaluated. He finds himself alone (and naked) in a hostile universe, where he cannot be certain of meaning and where the utter darkness of death seems imminent.

This existential dilemma perhaps recalls that of Oliver Winemiller— the hustler explicitly likened to a work of art, a statue from antiquity—who wanders the streets of various American cities in the short story "One Arm" (1948) and the screenplay with the same title, written in 1967. Disaffected and largely contemptuous of the so-called johns who seem attracted to his disability, Ollie learns, too late, of the love others feel for him and the impact he has made on their lives. Before that realization, Ollie (in the screenplay) objects to his client Lester's playing a country music record, a song with words that seem to be Williams's own and that anticipate *Le Solitaire*:

> Buildings seem much taller
> When you're going from a town.
> You see peculiar shadows
> But don't let 'em bring you down.
>
> If you had a buddy with you,
> I mean one that's tried an' true,
> I can tell you 'cause I know it,
> Shadows wouldn't be so blue. (250)

The search for a "buddy" is also a search for homosexual companionship, given that "the queer, the mutilated, the not-so-young-anymore" are "stifled to dumbness by the iron hand of bigotry and law" (253). Williams's painted figure may be in similar circumstances, even some seven years after Stonewall, though leaving the suffocating city would only seem to lessen his chances of gay experiences, take him away from a community with its own survival tactics.

Rebaptism

> As a matter of fact, I have been resurrected and come back to life.
> —Tennessee Williams, in an interview with Rex Reed (1971)

A consequence of Williams's public coming out seems to have been a greater willingness to confess, to expose himself more than was absolutely necessary—if not to seek some sense of absolution, then at least to titillate. His 1975 novel *Moise and the World of Reason* was, according to its editor, Michael Korda, "a kind of autobiographical peep show" (qtd. in Lahr 545) but, as John Lahr points out, was merely a foretaste of "the real striptease" that was the *Memoirs*, published in the same year (545).[8] Some of his other writing of the time engaged more earnestly with the nature of gay experience and the life it created. Quentin's well-known monologue in *Small Craft Warnings* (1972) is a case in point. Having lost the ability to be surprised, the character speaks of the "deadening coarseness" that is "the experience of most homosexuals" and then more graphically likens this life to "the jabbing of a hypodermic needle" (260); it is a numbing addiction devoid of interest, he contends. Quentin's remarks are by no means representative of those made by the dramatic characters post 1970, and we cannot say with any certainty that they are the views of the author: of note here is their general mood of confession, which characterizes Williams's written and visual works at the time and, importantly, is coincident with the renewal of his religious faith.

The paintings avoid gay sexual encounters, problematized or otherwise, but they do document a more personal confession after 1970, one analogous with Williams's renewed faith. His conversion to Catholicism in 1969, at the suggestion of his brother, Dakin, has been widely regarded as a sham, another symptom of his vulnerability and incoherent thinking. Yet, without dismissing his Episcopalian background completely, Williams insisted that it was not out of character: "I have always been a Catholic in my work," he wrote to his editor Robert MacGregor, and he describes being captivated by "the chanted Mass, and the rich ceremony" (qtd. in Lahr 491), although he remained unconvinced by the idea of immortality.

A useful site for tracking confession, spirituality, and faith as they play out in Williams's art is the water imagery that suffuses both the written and the visual work.[9] According to Philip C. Kolin, *Small Craft Warnings*, which creates a landscape between land and water, is one of a series of plays in which Williams—who, Kolin asserts, "repeatedly and consistently saw himself as a Christian writer" (110)—allegorizes spiritual conflicts through coastal settings. He harnesses this spirituality for his paintings of the seventies, too, though his figures do not seem to wrestle with their faith or enshrine the age-old binary opposition of flesh and spirit that was so much a feature of plays like *Summer and Smoke* (1948). Here, the conjunction of nudity with Christian iconography suggests not the guilt of transgressive sexual experience and identity so much as emotional honesty and the divestment of material trappings. Crucifixes abound, and Williams's watery settings (no doubt inspired by Key West locations like the entrepreneur David Wolkowsky's private island, Ballast Key, where he liked to paint) connote both untrammeled emotion and purification. Williams's aforementioned love of ritual, and the Mass in particular, is hinted at in carefully positioned tables that support drinking vessels: visual references to the Eucharist. The paintings, then, record inner contemplation and renewed commitment, not doubt or any incompatibility between Williams's religion and other aspects of his life. Unlike some of the roughly contemporary plays, they are not confessional so much as consolatory—an antidote to the funk of professional failure, the huge sense of loss following the death of Frank Merlo in 1963, and the alcohol and drug addiction that contributed to Williams's near-death experience in 1969. And yet consolation is not obviously coupled with Christian brotherhood and warmth of feeling. These paintings, like *Les Etrangers Amoureuses*, preserve the coldness and emotional distance of detachment. Only in *La Derniere* (sic) *Embrasse* (1977), a composition in which a man on bended knees clasps a woman's midriff as multicolored lines radiate from them, is there a

Fig. 3. *The Tidings Brought to Mary at Far Rockaway* (1975), by Tennessee Williams. Courtesy Key West Art and Historical Society, 2018.33.0085.

real sense of love and commitment, but there is no recognizable Christian context, and the title's eschatological theme only confirms Williams's skepticism about the afterlife: there is nothing beyond this last embrace.

Williams's invocation of Christian tradition and belief in his paintings can and should be considered a form of intertextuality: unsurprisingly, his visual art was nearly as explicitly intertextual as his writing, which features countless allusions to other writers, both in epigraphs and the bodies of his works. The paintings pictorialize scenes from his own writing (*Sulla Terrazza della Signora Stone*, "Lament for the Moths") and draw inspiration from other writers, such as Wallace Stevens. To see Williams's painting engaging explicitly with religion and text, one need only look at *The Tidings Brought to Mary at Far Rockaway* (fig. 3). The title and the subject refer to a drama by Paul Claudel (1868–1955): a highly allegorical, austere play of Christian miracles, *L'Annonce faite à Marie* or *The Tidings Brought to Mary* (1912), set in the medieval era toward the end of the Western Schism within the Catholic church. Williams's choice to use the Claudel play as a stimulus seems odd: its fervent prescription of self-sacrifice and abandonment of family, of expiating the sins of others and embracing death as the true meaning of life, seems difficult to correlate with many of his preoccupations; and Williams's attempt to update and partially secularize the play by locating it in the beach resort of Far Rockaway in the New York borough of Queens is perplexing. Are the figures in the painting based on real people that Williams knew, or are they versions of the characters in *The Tidings Brought to Mary*? Is the solemnization of their gathering an attempt to record a moment of overwhelming significance or merely a private joke (given that "Mary" has historically been a slang term for a feminine gay man)?

In the painting, a standing woman and a seated man appear in the foreground at center, separated on a diagonal plane by a coffee table that appears to support a crucifix, a cup and saucer, a glass, and a half-full bottle of wine. An apparently winged figure stands behind the woman, holding a gold crucifix in an arm that is extended in line with the woman's vision, though since he stands in the background, it is not clear whether or not the woman can see it. We cannot be certain whether this man is standing in a doorway or whether the somewhat incomplete orange frame—one of four "L" shapes or inverted sevens—around him encloses a picture of which he is the subject; either way, a gold halo complements his golden crucifix. Swirls of bold colors, some of which could be more figure sevens or even snakes, help to create a somewhat frenetic picture that belies the stillness and calm of the figures that appear to pose self-consciously, hands covering their genitalia.

They are arranged in an awkward triangle, further skewed by the perspective, one that perhaps represents the most important configuration of characters in Claudel's play: that of Anne Vercors, master of the estate; his eldest daughter, Violaine; and Pierre de Craon, who is working as a builder on the estate. Claudel's Anne leaves his family to make a pilgrimage to Jerusalem, to "the center and the navel of the world" (56), the site of the cross. This pilgrimage may be deemed—as it is initially by his wife, Elizabeth—a dereliction of duty, but Anne is acutely aware of two things: that France (and Western Europe more generally) has lost its way, and that those who have prospered have done so by the will of God. With no monarch in France and three popes vying for power in different locations, "everything is upset and put out of its right place" (52). By obeying the angel's trumpet and going to the Holy Land, Anne believes he is ensuring that "the portions may be distributed afresh" (55). Violaine, a figura Christi, "a symbol of eternity within time, of spirit within matter" (Fowlie 60), has been sexually assaulted before the action of the play commences. Her attacker, Craon, believes his leprosy is divine punishment, but Violaine forgives him with a kiss in the prologue to the play. Freed from his guilt and the bonds of his earthly love through her generous act (though the audience learns later that Violaine has contracted leprosy from the kiss), Craon is able to focus on his chief purpose: building cathedrals that express not only devotion to God but also "the unity of a people" (Giussani 13).

For many, Violaine is the pivotal figure in the play, a view seemingly confirmed by earlier versions entitled *La jeune fille Violaine*. She not only forms a triangle with the male characters already mentioned but also forms a triangle with her betrothed, Jacques Hury, and her sexually jealous sister, Mara. The critic Wallace Fowlie claims that Violaine's mysticism is analogous to that of a poet, who (as conceived by Claudel) has to achieve "a deep inner silence" that comes from detachment from the world (60). The blond woman in Williams's painting could be Violaine: her radiance and blue eyes recall the heroine, and her position in front of a saint or angel (who could be either Pierre or Anne—or neither) indicates a privileged status. However, the viewer's eye is also drawn to a bold blue cross or frame centrally placed in the upper portion of the picture. The cross's position separates the figures further, creating, as in the paintings mentioned earlier, a composition of two halves, perhaps an acknowledgment of the separation that characterizes much of Claudel's play. But the cross's color unifies: the same blue provides a heavy outline for each of the figures, the seated man's chair, and another frame behind his head; two blocks of blue presumably serve as flooring or carpet but also suggest water in which the figures paddle their feet. The pools of blue (possibly a nod to the beach landscapes of Edward Henry Potthast [1857–1927], perhaps the most famous images of Far Rockaway) help to break up the dominant flesh color, creating a series of interconnected islands. They might also represent Violaine's extended influence: in Claudel's play, Violaine miraculously brings her sister's baby back to life, in the process making its previously black eyes blue.

While the pink, mauve, and orange colors in the painting denote earthiness, the gold accents create an ethereal glow, shared by all three figures but originating with the one at the back, whose halo and crucifix radiate golden light and whose upper body seems bathed in it. The crucifixes themselves are also arranged in a loose "L" shape, the third being that emblazoned on the seated figure's chest and confirming that this scene is about spiritual transcendence rather than sexuality, though perhaps the two are not incompatible.

Williams seems to have found Claudel's play not only consoling and uplifting in its miracles and piety but also intriguing in its triangulations. Interestingly, a more secular version of the configuration explored in *The Tidings Brought to Mary at Far Rockaway* can be found in an untitled painting of 1976. In this piece, two burly, topless male figures occupy the center of the picture while a naked woman stands suggestively, hand on hip, in a doorway. A larger table is positioned between the men, not as a form of altar as it is in *The Tidings Brought to Mary* but as part of a bar or brothel (a brothel being more likely, given that the word *pussy* is scrawled above the table between the men). Again, there is no obvious communication between the figures—they merely furnish the room as much as a Victrola that is to the left of the men and in front of the woman—and we are left to speculate on their precise relationships and what is about to take place. By simply changing the arrangement of men and women, replacing the haloed man with a brazen woman, Williams has created two versions of what is essentially the same scene, one earthly and one spiritual. What remains the same is the lack of connectivity between the figures, an apartness that cannot be alleviated by either sex or religion. Though the color blue works to unite the figures in *The Tidings* by way of the cross, it cannot finally break down the islands on which each seems stranded. While the table is shared by the men in the untitled painting, a light shade is suspended over their heads, almost as sure a mark of division as the tree that separates Williams from his mother in *On ne peut pas comprendre toujours*, and the woman seems as trapped by her arched doorway as she is keen to parade her sexuality.

An Intimate Mirror

> The act of painting is an intimate mirror. I think Tennessee
> Williams liked the reflection he discovered in his work.
> —William Andrews, qtd. in Mark Guarino, "A New Orleans
> Exhibit Shows a Side of Tennessee Williams Few Knew: Painter"

The most interesting paintings of this period play out a drama of irreconcilability and uncertainty, the plastic spaces between Williams's figures serving to emphasize their separation and disconnection. Contrary to what Terri Smith Ruckel suggests, coexistence on the same plane, connection via invisible lines, and symmetry are not conditions that, by themselves, mark the splitting or doubling of a similar figure. Yes, Williams was interested in androgyny, as demonstrated by his choice to name not only a poem but his entire second collection of poetry *Androgyne, Mon Amour* (1977), but, pictorially, androgyny is usually captured in the feminine features of a man, like the standing figure in *Les Etrangers Amoureuses* or the seated subject of *Citizen of World III: Set for Target Practise*. He is not painting men and women who are elements of one person wrenched apart, though staging his characters as bifurcations of a whole (e.g., in a play such as *In the Bar of a Tokyo Hotel*) can be plausible and compelling.

Too much emphasis on androgyny can also underplay the individual strength women exhibit in some of the paintings. While Williams's female subjects may appear subdued, such as the woman with a downturned head standing behind the proxemically dominant man in the painting *Many Moons Ago*, the woman in *La Derniere Embrasse*, for example, stands like an earth mother, seemingly the only source of consolation for the kneeling man. Of the three people crowded into the small central space of *Nus*, it is only the woman who faces us, her hand hovering over a crucifix. In *She Sang beyond the Genius of the Sea* (1975), the central figure is a woman holding aloft a trident, almost proclaiming a new world order as the men on either side of her stand further back in lesser roles. And, as we have seen, the blond in *The Tidings Brought to Mary at Far Rockaway* occupies a pivotal position in the foreground of the painting that makes her a conduit to the spiritual world, a means of salvation.

Nevertheless, men still outnumber women in Williams's paintings from the seventies. In some instances, a single subject poses provocatively in a manner that suggests availability. For example, in *Antinous in Repose* (1977), *Mister Paradise*, *La Langue Perdue*, and *Citizen of World III: Set for Target Practise*, the male subjects are unguarded and centrally positioned, almost unequivocally objects of desire. The style bears out a somewhat shameful longing for both youth and youths, a tongue-in-cheek admission that, as Blanche DuBois recognizes in her corruption of boys, "I've got to be good—and keep my hands off children" (*Streetcar* 339). By contrast, *Lament for the Moths* (1978), based on his poem of the same title, shows Williams working with a more serious purpose and more mature style. The subject, a centrally positioned, alluring man, poses supine, his eyes closed and his left arm dangling; he appears suspended, seemingly abandoned by the world. He is one of the "velvety moths" Williams refers to in the poem ("Lament"). And yet the brutality of Williams's poem, with its semantic field of disease and destruction ("plague," "stricken," "pestilent," "invisible evil," "treacherous killer") and the "mammoth figures" that haunt its "heavy world," is hardly recognizable in the painting. The luscious composition, a mass of barely distinguishable shapes in a warm palette of pink, blue, and yellow swirling around the figure, suggests that, far from being destroyed by a toxic miasma, the mothlike man has been preserved in beautiful splendor. Loneliness is his indulgence, one that the isolated viewer can appreciate.

Williams's homoerotic art, then, seems designed to titillate, to share the artist's appreciation of the male form with his subjects and the paintings' prospective owners. But Williams's gaze is rarely merely voyeuristic: the works display various types of pictorial narrative that provoke the big questions posed by his drama—about sexual politics, the nature of our spiritual lives, and the profound isolation of the human condition. He painted his nudes, yes, but generally with a surprising restraint or modesty that avoids the "quality of excess" the artist and art historian Jonathan Weinberg notes in several American male artists' representations of men (*Male Desire* 9). Invariably, it is more instructive to look beyond the bared flesh to the vulnerability and emotional integrity it connotes, to the depths of character Williams understood so well. As he told David Wolkowsky, the owner of several of the paintings discussed here, Williams painted not the surface likeness but what he saw beneath, not "the physical you, but the spirit visible to me."[10]

Notes

[1] Lyle Leverich claims that Mabie referred to Williams as "that pansy" (237); Williams remarks in *Memoirs* that "Mabie was prejudiced against me and against Lemuel Ayers" (49).

[2] Williams was even prepared to borrow the titles and subjects of well-known paintings: his 1938 play *American Gothic* was a case in point. According to John S. Bak, Williams "poached" not only the title of Grant Wood's 1930 *American Gothic* but also its iconic couple to write a play that was not so much about themes in Wood's painting as it was an effort to work through some of the problems he was encountering with the writing of *Fugitive Kind* ("*American Gothic*" 175).

[3] Such high praise would also seem to confirm a correspondence between Hofmann's theory of plasticity—the idea that a painting can become a three-dimensional experience as a result of the tension between its different elements—and Williams's concept of plastic theater (outlined in his production notes to *The Glass Menagerie*). For a fuller discussion of this topic, see Richard E. Kramer's essay "'The Sculptural Drama': Tennessee Williams's Plastic Theatre."

[4] As well as featuring in the permanent collection at the Key West Art and Historical Society, paintings by Williams have been exhibited at the Ogden Museum of Southern Art in New Orleans (7 Mar.–31 May 2015) and the St. Louis University Museum of Art (5 May–23 July 2017). A small number of Williams's paintings, given to the Australian painter Michael Garady, appeared in an exhibition at the St. Giles Street Gallery in Norwich, England (24 Oct.–27 Nov. 2008).

[5] *The Fleet's In!* was famously removed from the Corcoran Gallery of Art in Washington, DC, at the insistence of a retired admiral, Hugh Rodman. The stated objection was not to its homoeroticism but to the painting's depiction of drunken, brawling sailors, a gross misrepresentation of the service as Rodman saw it. However, Richard Meyer feels that the inclusion of an obviously homosexual figure among the sailors "was almost certainly a factor in the picture's censorship" (54).

[6] Jonathan Weinberg postulates that Demuth's more outrageous paintings "were probably done to please himself or, at the most, a select group of friends" (*Speaking* 53).

[7] In 1973, Williams joked with an interviewer about his preference for androgynous men: "I mean I'm only attracted to androgynous males, like Garbo. Ha! After a few drinks, I can't distinguish between the two. [. . . W]omen aren't as likely as the androgynous male to give you sexual reassurance" ("*Playboy* Interview" 229).

[8] Korda's comment originally appeared in his 22 Mar. 1999 *New Yorker* article "That's It, Baby."

[9] Water imagery also features significantly in events surrounding his conversion. E.g., his conversion took place in Key West, at the appropriately named St. Mary Star of the Sea Catholic Church, and he was given a copy of Thomas Merton's *No Man Is an Island* (1955) by the officiating Jesuit priest, Father Joseph LeRoy.

[10] Williams's portrait of Wolkowsky, *L'inconnu: C'est les Yeux* (1981), caused the sitter some consternation. Rather than tear the portrait up, as Wolkowsky commanded, Williams wrote on the back: "Dear David, you realize I wasn't painting the physical you, but the spirit visible to me. Love, Tennessee" (qtd. in Guarino).

Works Cited

Bak, John S. "*American Gothic* Grants Tennessee Williams a 'Woodian' Play." *Philological Quarterly*, vol. 88, nos. 1–2, Spring 2009, pp. 171–84.

——. *Tennessee Williams: A Literary Life*. Palgrave Macmillan, 2013.

Boxill, Roger. *Tennessee Williams*. Macmillan, 1987.

Claudel, Paul. *The Tidings Brought to Mary*. Human Adventure, 2009.

Devlin, Albert J., editor. *Conversations with Tennessee Williams*. UP of Mississippi, 1986.

Fowlie, Wallace. *Paul Claudel*. Bowes, 1957.

Garady, Michael. "Tennessee Williams: A Portrait of the Playwright as Painter." Interview by Chris Wiegand. *The Guardian*, 24 Oct. 2008, www.theguardian.com/culture/2008/oct/24/art-theatre-tennessee-williams. Accessed 10 Dec. 2018.

Giussani, Luigi. Introduction. Claudel, pp. 9–20.

Guarino, Mark. "A New Orleans Exhibit Shows a Side of Tennessee Williams Few Knew: Painter." *Washington Post*, 10 Apr. 2015.

House, Charles. *The Outrageous Life of Henry Faulkner: Portrait of an Appalachian Artist*. U of Tennessee P, 1988.

Isaac, Dan. Introduction. *Spring Storm*, by Tennessee Williams, New Directions, 1999, pp. vii–xxv.

Kolin, Philip C. "'Having Lost the Ability to Say: "My God!"': The Theology of Tennessee Williams's *Small Craft Warnings*." *The Undiscovered Country: The Later Plays of Tennessee Williams*, edited by Kolin, Lang, 2002, pp. 107–24.

Kramer, Richard E. "The Sculptural Drama: Tennessee Williams' Plastic Theatre." *Tennessee Williams Annual Review*, vol. 5, 2002, www.tennesseewilliamsstudies.org/journal/work.php?ID=45.

Lahr, John. *Tennessee Williams: Mad Pilgrimage of the Flesh*. Bloomsbury, 2014.

Leverich, Lyle. *Tom: The Unknown Tennessee Williams*. Norton, 1995.

Maruéjouls-Koch, Sophie. "Tennessee Williams and Jackson Pollock: The Art of Crossing the Line." *Tennessee Williams Annual Review*, vol. 14, 2014, pp. 22–49.

Meyer, Richard. *Outlaw Representation: Censorship and Homosexuality in Twentieth-Century American Art*. Oxford UP, 2002.

Pearlstein, Philip. "Figure Paintings Today Are Not Made in Heaven." *ARTnews*, vol. 61, no. 4, Summer 1962, pp. 39, 51–52.

Plumley, William. "Tennessee Williams's Graphic Art: 'Two on a Party.'" *Mississippi Quarterly*, vol. 48, no. 4, Fall 1995, pp. 789–805.

Ristić, Ivan. "The Male Gaze: Intimate Proximity and Desire." *Nude Men: From 1800 to the Present Day*, edited by Tobias G. Natter and Elisabeth Leopold, Hirmer, 2012, pp. 286–99.

Smith Ruckel, Terri. "*Ut Pictura Poesis, Ut Poesis Pictura*: The Painterly Texture of Tennessee Williams's *In the Bar of a Tokyo Hotel*." *The Undiscovered Country: The Later Plays of Tennessee Williams*, edited by Philip C. Kolin, Lang, 2002, pp. 80–92.

Vidal, Gore. "Some Memories of the Glorious Bird and an Earlier Self." *United States: Essays 1952–1992*, Abacus, 2010, pp. 1131–48.

Weinberg, Jonathan. *Male Desire: The Homoerotic in American Art*. Abrams, 2004.

——. *Speaking for Vice: Homosexuality in the Art of Charles Demuth, Marsden Hartley, and the First American Avant-Garde*. Yale UP, 1993.

Williams, Tennessee. "An Appreciation of Hans Hofmann." Williams, *New Selected Essays*, pp. 197–98.

——. *Battle of Angels*. Williams, *Theatre*, vol. 1, pp. 1–122.

——. "The Dangerous Painters." *The Collected Poems of Tennessee Williams*, edited by David Roessel and Nicholas Moschovakis, New Directions, 2002, pp. 38–43.

——. "Lament for the Moths." *The Collected Poems of Tennessee Williams*, edited by David Roessel and Nicholas Moschovakis, New Directions, 2002, p. 17.

——. *Memoirs*. Doubleday, 1975.

——. *Moise and the World of Reason*. Simon and Schuster, 1975.

——. *New Selected Essays: Where I Live*. Edited by John S. Bak, New Directions, 2009.

——. *The Night of the Iguana*. Williams, *Theatre*, vol. 4, pp. 247–376.

——. *One Arm*. Stopped Rocking *and Other Screenplays*, New Directions, 1984, pp. 193–291.

——. "The Past, the Present, and the Perhaps." Williams, *New Selected Essays*, pp. 79–82.

——. "*Playboy* Interview: Tennessee Williams." 1973. Interview with C. Robert Jennings. Devlin, pp. 224–50.

——. *The Selected Letters of Tennessee Williams, Volume 1, 1920–1945*. Edited by Albert J. Devlin and Nancy M. Tischler, Oberon, 2001.

——. *Small Craft Warnings*. Williams, *Theatre*, vol. 5, pp. 215–300.

——. *A Streetcar Named Desire*. Williams, *Theatre*, vol. 1, pp. 239–419.

——. "Tennessee Williams Turns Sixty." 1971. Interview with Rex Reed. Devlin, pp. 184–207.

——. *The Theatre of Tennessee Williams*. New Directions, 1971–92. 8 vols.

——. "The Timeless World of a Play." Williams, *New Selected Essays*, pp. 59–62.

——. *Will Mr. Merriwether Return from Memphis?* The Traveling Companion *and Other Plays*, edited by Annette J. Saddik, New Directions, 2008, pp. 225–86.

Recent Releases

R. Barton Palmer

*His Other Life: Searching for My Father, His First Wife, and
Tennessee Williams.* By Melanie McCabe. U of New
Orleans P, 2017, 252 pages.

*The Luck of Friendship: The Letters of Tennessee Williams and
James Laughlin.* Edited by Peggy L. Fox and Thomas
Keith. W. W. Norton, 2018, 432 pages.

F ew would argue that the writer's life does not inform the oeuvre in
which it is slantwise contained. However, what we mean exactly by
"informs" merits some discussion in a review of two books that, in
quite different ways, contribute to the life-writing devoted to Tennessee
Williams.

The record of a writer's life is not simply a nexus of existential facts
but a culturally shaped, multiply authored, and always evolving text. In
large part, the life is produced by the painstaking work of biographical
critics, for whose mill the author's works routinely figure as a kind of grist.
Mining the oeuvre for materials to fill in the blanks in the record requires
discernment and caution from the biographer. When fiction incorporates
the real, it does so on its own terms. Doubtless, the life partly constituted
from reading the works has considerable value as a portrait of the artist.
But what role, if any, should the life text play in the primary task of literary criticism, which is to assess the meaning and value of what the author
has written? The novelist Milan Kundera, for one, questions the value
of attempting to bring the two universes, one experiential and the other
fabulized, into productive alignment. Reading works from the perspective

of the author's life, Kundera suggests, is only a pointless unmaking of the formalizing energies that composed those works in the first place:

> According to a well-known metaphor, the novelist demolishes the house of his life and uses its bricks to construct another house: that of his novel. From which it follows that a novelist's biographers unmake what the novelist made, and remake what he unmade. Their labor, from the standpoint of art utterly negative, can illuminate neither the value nor the meaning of a novel. (146)

As Kundera sees it, literary biography is of no use to the critic, who should be satisfied with the oeuvre tout court. If based in part on the writings, the life is a misguided rebuilding of a rebuilding. Inevitably, such a biography is two Platonic removes from the "lived"—or, at least, from the lived-life as it appears in the form that holds the highest value for any reader: namely, the text that the artist built from his or her life. What use is biography to the critic if it sheds no light on the works from which it is in part drawn? Kundera has a point: absent the textual legacy of impressive breadth and aesthetic power, not to mention the deep cultural relevance of the playwright's career, we would not be particularly interested in the life of a certain Tom Williams who grew up in St. Louis, Missouri. That said, Kundera goes too far in insisting that the labor of literary biographers is "utterly negative" in its relation to art and to the analytical or evaluative work of criticism. He is, of course, hardly an unbiased source for this view; most, if not all, authors would like the inevitable messiness of their lives to have nothing to do with how their work is evaluated.

It is worth remembering that the author's life, as Boris Tomashevsky argues, "operates in the reader's consciousness" and may be considered a "traditional concomitant to artistic work" (47). The life can supplement a text's meaning, adding an extratextual dimension that the author may even have intended. There are always intriguing (dis)connections between the artist made known to readers through his or her life and the artist revealed indirectly—often tantalizingly—in the works. Such a measuring of selves—often explicitly invited by the author—is difficult to resist as a form of reading. "The truth is," the literary biographer Leon Edel reminds us, "that, however much we may isolate a picture on a wall and try to keep our eyes within its frame, we do not wholly lose our awareness of the wall or the adjacent pictures." As Edel admonishes, "the literary voice is not one of the 'voices of silence'; it cannot be separated [. . .] from the speaker or from the listening world" (xiii). Most important, considered in all its various aspects and constructed from a wide casting of investigative nets for materials, the author's life often sheds important light on the various acts of composition that make up the author's career. The history of the writer as a writer has for good reason always been central to author studies, challenged but never discredited by approaches to meaning and hence value that have come and gone, reflecting fleeting fashions embraced by literary scholars. Interestingly, Kundera makes the point that the literary world is more interested in biographical interpretations of Kafka's oeuvre than in the author's rather unusually ordinary life. And yet, he acknowledges that the Kafka phenomenon—that is, the proliferation of biographical approaches to Kafka's work—emerges from readers' extraordinary interest in authors' lives in general and the use of the life as a critical tool.

For the purposes of this discussion, let us assume that the focus of literary commentary should be authorship, a nexus of different concerns (aesthetic, professional, contextual) that straddles the border we usually draw between the life, broadly conceived, and the textual legacy. A key point about Williams is that he was conscious of this border. He never followed other writers in the postwar era (Norman Mailer and Philip Roth come immediately to mind) in adopting a metafictional narcissism that puts a semi-fictionalized version of the author at the center of a work. His Tom Wingfield in *The Glass Menagerie*, though sharing so many elements of Williams's life, is not the explicit authorial stand-in at the center of a pseudo-autobiographical fiction such as Mailer's *Armies of the Night* (1968) or Roth's *The Counterlife* (1986). In Mailer's and Roth's works, what was originally extradiegetic (the author producing a work for readers) becomes diegetic, as textual insides and outsides change places. The writer becomes a character, while the extratextual facticity of his compositional career becomes partly material for the tale. Once textualized, such writing is inevitably poised unstably between auto- and pseudo-autobiography no matter how "true" it might be. Rhetorically speaking, nothing Williams wrote is *à clef* in this manner (or even in the less insistent autobiographical modes of a Hemingway or Fitzgerald). "Williams" must be searched out in his work in a different way. Aside from the important role that his sister, Rose, and his mother played as models for key characters, especially in the early plays, his presence proves vague, elusive, and fleeting, as Melanie McCabe demonstrates at some length in her study of a teenaged Williams's possibly formative relationship with a peer during high school.

In *His Other Life*, McCabe discusses how the girl on whom Tennessee Williams had a crush in late adolescence, Hazel Kramer, as well as the young man she eventually, and disastrously, married (McCabe's father, Terrence), have left marginal traces in the playwright's work. Most of the relevant facts on the timeline have been identified by earlier biographers, but McCabe's indefatigable research has enabled her to augment the names and dates with sympathetic reconstructions of these relationships. McCabe offers readers an engaging and densely detailed account of her years-long project tracing her family roots, and an all-too-often banal subject is enlivened here by its unusual focus. She is mostly interested in discovering what she can of the relationship of her father, Terrence M. McCabe, to his first wife, Hazel Kramer, whom he divorced. Terrence's first marriage, McCabe reports, was a subject mentioned rarely and always obliquely, never discussed at length within the family from his successful second marriage. McCabe learns about her father's first marriage and his ex-wife's connection to Williams only when, at seventeen, she pries the relevant details from her reluctant mother. Hazel Kramer's connection with Williams, and to some degree with Terrence, propels McCabe to learn more (and provides a hook, at least of sorts, for the book).

Williams, in his *Memoirs*, reveals that the cardiovascular troubles he suffered in his early twenties might have had their origin in his breakup with Kramer and then her marriage to Terrence. The daughter feels a certain pride (subsequently making it part of her life story) that her father "had caused the renowned Tennessee Williams to have a heart attack" (17). But, leaving aside this overblown medical drama, the story of Hazel and Tom seems to have more or less ended at this point; McCabe's evidence that this friendship continued is not particularly persuasive. To be fair, McCabe did not have much to work with: it would be a stretch to say that, beyond their brief and never consummated love affair (if that is indeed what it should be called), Hazel Kramer played any significant role in Williams's life.

Kramer's story, to be sure, is the stuff of melodrama, and McCabe effectively relates the details, insofar as she can discover them. Miserable after the divorce that ended her relationship with Terrence and disappointed by her inability to press her claim to family assets, Kramer became increasingly unhinged. The downward spiral ended when, at only thirty-eight, she swallowed a handful of Seconal in a shabby Mexican hotel room. *His Other Life* turns out to be a *triste histoire* of a young woman who never made a success of her adult life enlisting an old friend to testify in an ultimately failed attempt to secure her financial future. Williams, at Kramer's request, testified that Kramer's grandmother intended to leave Kramer a substantial portion of her estate, then currently in probate. The now-successful playwright apparently wrote to support Kramer's claim, but the letter has disappeared from the record. No other correspondence between the two is extant. If he was distressed by the news of her suicide, there is no record of his reaction, suggesting that Kramer was little more than a distant memory. McCabe's search to prove a deeper connection ends in frustration. In regard to Kramer's tragic death in squalid circumstances, the author notes, "I have found nothing in his letters or journal entries. This seems to me nothing short of incredible" (246). Well, not really; the omission isn't strange if Kramer's passing barely registered. Years later, in writing *The Red Devil Battery Sign*, Williams named one of the characters Terrence McCabe, but, beyond the use of her father's name, McCabe can discover little resonance between the life model and this fictional construction. As Kundera might put it, the "bricks" of life from which a writer makes his or her house of fiction are often just bricks, not messages to be decoded.

His Other Life has only small beer to offer Williams scholars or aficionados. It is largely a memoir devoted to McCabe's energetic and persistent effort to learn the details of her father's life. That the book includes in its prefatory materials a family tree of the McCabe and Kramer families is a warning of sorts to readers who might be expecting the book to focus on Tennessee Williams. McCabe eventually decides that she has learned as much as can be learned, which is, as she confesses in her conclusion, that she now has a "rounder, fuller picture of the father I lost so early in life" (252). As a memoir (and as a recounting of the story of its composition), *His Other Life* succeeds admirably. McCabe has the successful biographer's talent for organizing masses of detail and keeping a clear narrative through line.

In their edition of the correspondence between Williams and the New Directions publisher James Laughlin, Peggy L. Fox and Thomas Keith provide the raw materials of a "joint story" that, Fox concedes, is "only a small part of the life of either man" (xiii). The story of their professional friendship, easily read out from the correspondence, is one very much worth telling and, now fleshed out with a treasure trove of reminiscences, comments, and wry interchanges, finds an important place in the evolving text of the playwright's life. *The Luck of Friendship* has been much reviewed, with Simon Callow's appreciative notice in the *New York Review of Books*, "Tenn's Best Friend" (27 Sept. 2018), emphasizing one aspect— the personal—of the biographical information in these letters. From the viewpoint of Williams studies, however, this edition has another and quite different value. The Williams letters, as Fox suggests, speak eloquently to "his willingness to do what was necessary to be a professional writer across several genres" (xiii).

Like the three volumes of Williams correspondence edited by Albert Devlin and Nancy Tischler, *The Luck of Friendship* contains much that future researchers will find invaluable. The interchanges between Williams and Laughlin often take up those issues of composition (the whys and wherefores of how the writer spends his creative energies at different moments) that are so central to the chronicling of his professional career. *The Luck of Friendship* provides ample substance for a life-and-works approach to contextualizing the oeuvre, in which the author's recorded opinions about his intentions provide important evidence. Fox and Keith's offerings to the community of Williams scholars will have enduring value for that important critical task.

If Hazel Kramer played only a small role in the life of Tennessee Williams, James Laughlin was a central figure. He oversaw one of the several streams of publication (broadly considered) and income that constituted Williams's professional career, the activity on which the playwright depended to create—and then sustain—a lifestyle of some affluence and flexibility. Because Laughlin was his publisher, Williams was prompted often to write to him about matters more connected to the business than to the art of writing. One of the major themes of the correspondence collected here is the difficulty of maintaining writing as a sole career—that is, of earning enough money through writing to support oneself without engaging in other forms of employment. The Williams-Laughlin correspondence speaks indirectly to the exceptional opportunities for earning that were available to dramatists like Williams. Fees for stage production were dwarfed by the comparatively huge amounts available for the sale of screen rights to Hollywood, while the transformation of playscripts into play texts—the task of New Directions—provided both another source of income and literary prestige.

The business acumen that Williams often demonstrated in managing his long career comes through clearly in these letters. In a 1950 exchange, for example, the playwright, still at the beginning of what would become a string of successes, comments incisively on the situation of his friend the novelist Paul Bowles, who had recently chosen to abandon Laughlin and New Directions for Bennett Cerf. Bowles, Williams observes, "is not a quick or facile writer" and is "not going to turn out a best seller every season, and he is worried about bread and butter until the next really good book is ready. [. . .] Cerf offers him a kind of subsidy" (151). Is this an oblique hint that New Directions might consider providing him with something similar, or a pointed observation that the financial relationships between publishers and their most important clients took place within a marketplace where writers would be best advised to pursue their main chance? Many of the letters in this edition invite this kind of reading. Laughlin and Williams may have been lucky enough to find friendship in their connection, but that connection, particularly for a writer constantly (and rightly) concerned about his earning potential, was based on economics.

Fox hints in her introduction that the Laughlin-Williams relationship provides a "window into the literary history of the twentieth-century" (xiii). The letters do provide such a window, but the book's full potential for illuminating this broader concern is not identified by the editors, who, with their own eye perhaps on the marketplace, are more interested in making this a book about Tennessee Williams. The fact is that *The Luck of Friendship* is but one in a series of expertly presented editions of Laughlin's correspondence with the different writers he handled during his long career at New Directions. Included in the James Laughlin Selected Letters series are volumes devoted to Guy Davenport, Thomas Merton, Henry Miller, Ezra Pound, Delmore Schwartz, Kenneth Rexroth, and William Carlos Williams. Edited by an interesting cast of scholars, the texts constitute an impressive roster of twentieth-century literary lights. The purpose of the project is the preservation of the material legacy, presumably assembled from the publisher's files, that is Laughlin's career, which, as these volumes outline, is every bit as worthy of note as that of the famous Scribner's editors Maxwell Perkins and John Hall Wheelock. Thanks to New Directions and W. W. Norton, Laughlin's correspondence in its entirety, and not just the Tennessee Williams volume, makes it possible for critics and historians to assess the editor's important place in twentieth-century literary history, of which his relationship with Tennessee Williams is but one chapter, albeit an interesting and especially rich one.

Works Cited

Edel, Leon. *Literary Biography*. 1957. Anchor Books, 1959.
Kundera, Milan. *The Art of the Novel*. 1986. HarperCollins, 1986.
Tomashevsky, Boris. "Literature and Biography." *Readings in Russian Poetics*, edited by Ladislav Matejka and Krystyna Pomorska, MIT Press, 1971, pp. 42–53.

Notes on Contributors

John S. Bak is professor at the Université de Lorraine in France, where he teaches courses in literary journalism and American drama and theater. His articles on Williams have appeared in such journals as *Theatre Journal*, *Mississippi Quarterly*, *Journal of American Drama and Theatre*, the *Tennessee Williams Literary Journal*, *American Drama*, *South Atlantic Review*, and *Studies in Musical Theatre*. His edited books include *Post/modern Dracula: From Victorian Themes to Postmodern Praxis* (2007), *New Selected Essays: Where I Live* (2009), and, with Bill Reynolds, *Literary Journalism across the Globe: Journalistic Traditions and Transnational Influences* (2011). He is the author of the monographs *Homo Americanus: Ernest Hemingway, Tennessee Williams, and Queer Masculinities* (2010) and *Tennessee Williams: A Literary Life* (2013).

Michael S. D. Hooper is an independent scholar and private tutor. He is the author of *Sexual Politics in the Work of Tennessee Williams: Desire over Protest* (2012) and several essays in the *Tennessee Williams Annual Review*, and he is the editor of the Methuen Student Edition of *A Streetcar Named Desire* (2009). He wrote the Williams entry for the online *Routledge Encyclopedia of Modernism* (2016) and has contributed to *A Student Handbook to the Plays of Tennessee Williams*, edited by Katherine Weiss (2014). His essay "Pedro Almodóvar's Homage to Tennessee Williams" appears in *Tennessee Williams in Europe: Intercultural Encounters, Transatlantic Exchanges*, edited by John S. Bak (2014).

Tom Mitchell is associate professor of theatre at the University of Illinois, Urbana-Champaign. He has staged productions of six of Tennessee Williams's earliest full-length plays, including the twenty-first-century premieres of *Stairs to the Roof* and *Candles to the Sun.*

R. Barton Palmer is Calhoun Lemon Professor of Literature and director of the World Cinema program at Clemson University. He is the general editor of book series at six academic presses, including Palgrave Studies in Adaptation and Visual Culture, for which he has recently coedited (with Marc C. Conner) *Screening Modern Irish Fiction and Drama* (2016) and (with Julie Grossman) *Adaptation in Visual Culture: Images, Texts, and Their Multiple Worlds* (2017). His works on film adaptation include *Modern American Drama on Screen* (2013) and *Modern British Drama on Screen* (2013), both coedited with Robert Bray. He is the coauthor (with Bray) of *Hollywood's Tennessee: The Williams Films and Postwar America* (2009). His latest film book is *Shot on Location: Postwar American Cinema and the Exploration of Real Place* (2016). He is coeditor (with Conner) of *Screening Modern Irish Fiction and Drama* (2016) and coeditor (with Homer Pettey) of both *Rule, Britannia!: The Biopic and British National Identity* (2018) and *French Literature on Screen* (forthcoming).

Julie Vatain-Corfdir is associate professor of English at Sorbonne Université. Her research focuses on the dramatic text—on the page, on stage, and in translation. She is the author of a monograph on dramatic translation (*Traduire la lettre vive* [2012], winner of the SAES/AFEA book of the year award in 2013) and has edited or coedited *Lectures de Tom Stoppard: Arcadia* (2011), *La scène en version originale* (2015), and *American Musicals from Stage to Screen* (2019). She has published essays on British and United States theater and has translated into French plays by Thornton Wilder; Tina Howe; Henry Arthur Jones and Henry Herman; Susan Glaspell; and Sarah Ruhl. She is a coeditor of the e-Theatrum Mundi series for Sorbonne Université Presses.